FEARLESS

PRO HOCKEY'S
MOST FEARLESS
(AND FEARED) PLAYERS

Murray Townsend

photography by Dan Hamilton

W
Warwick Publishing
Toronto Chicago
www.warwickgp.com

Contents

Introduction

Don Cherry was beside himself.

Actually, he was beside Ron MacLean on his Coach's Corner segment during the intermission of *Hockey Night in Canada*, showing a clip from that night's playoff game.

You could tell he was excited because the decibel level in his voice rose as he went along.

Chris Simon, of the Washington Capitals, had picked up the puck in the corner and waltzed out in front of the net completely untouched, firing the puck past the Pittsburgh goalie.

Not only did nobody touch him, but nobody even came near him.

And why was that?

Because they were afraid of him, explained Cherry.

Simon might be the most feared player in the NHL, as well as being among the most fearless. A double whammy for opposing players. Simon looks the part, too, with his long hair, hardened features, and his 6′4″, 235-pound frame.

Size matters, but it isn't everything.

Theoren Fleury is 10 inches shorter and more than 50 pounds lighter, but he's not afraid of Chris Simon. In fact, he's not afraid of anybody or anything.

If he was, he wouldn't have scored one point in the NHL, much less over 900.

Even as a junior, despite leading the Western Hockey League with 160 points, to go with his 235 penalty minutes, NHL teams were afraid of him. But not the way Fleury would have liked. He didn't get chosen until 166th overall in the 1987 draft.

You could argue that Fleury's size made him fearless out of necessity.

He wouldn't be the only player in that category.

Toronto's Darcy Tucker is only 5′10″, small by today's NHL standards, but his heart probably puts him in the top ten in the league. Teammate Tie Domi is the same size, but is one of the league's most feared fighters.

Being fearless comes in many different forms.

What about the defensemen who throw themselves in front of 100-mile-per-hour slapshots?

Why? Why do they do that? It can't be much fun.

They can't help themselves, it's as simple as that. They block the shot, sometimes with their face, and sometimes with dire consequences, and they don't learn a thing. The next time on the ice they're tossing their bodies in front of those shots again.

When they're not sacrificing themselves for the team, they're battling the opposition's toughest players in front of their net and in the corners. They can't back down for even a moment. If an opposing bruiser even smells fear, it's lights out, in more ways than one.

Goaltenders have considerably more protection than the days when Johnny Bower was flopping all over the ice without a mask and Glenn Hall was being physically ill prior to every game. But the shots are a lot harder and higher and the game a lot faster.

No professional goaltender is afraid of shots coming in his direction. If he was, he would have changed positions when he was a kid. But a goaltender needs to be fearless just the same.

His position carries the most pressure of any position, probably in any professional sport. Nobody is saddled with the same level of responsibility for his team's success.

A goaltender must be fearless mentally, as well as physically. He can't let a bad game bite into his confidence, he can't pay attention to the boos from the crowd when he lets in a weak goal, and he can't let it get to him when the sportswriter suggests he can't cut it in the playoffs.

If Ron Tugnutt ever listened to what people said about him, he wouldn't have persevered after being discarded by team after team. He wouldn't have been able to lead the NHL with a 1.79 goals against average for Ottawa in the 1998–99 season.

Even then, he was traded the next season to Pittsburgh for Tom Barrasso, a more seasoned NHL playoff goalie, the Senators figured. While Barrasso was on the sidelines after six games, all Tugnutt did was lead the underdog Penguins to a first round victory over Washington, and top all goaltenders in goals against average and save percentage.

If you wanted to pick the most fearless player of our time, you wouldn't be wrong if you selected Mark Messier. A little long in the tooth now, and his scor-

ing numbers have diminished, but he still plays every game as if it were his last, and he still considers the puck his personal property. You mess with him and you still pay the price. Scott Stevens is another player in the same mold. They don't even know what fear means, and their age has no bearing on it.

Finally, there is another breed of fearless player in the NHL. We often refer to them as power forwards. They're the type who can put the puck in the net, will drop the gloves if necessary, and would go into a pit full of rattlesnakes if the puck was there and come out with it unscathed.

They command an intimidating presence when they're on the ice, in more ways than one. They're the guys you look to in the dying minutes of a close contest or during the playoffs. They're the type of player every kid wants to be when they make it to the NHL.

Owen Nolan of the San Jose Sharks is arguably the game's current premier power forward. He had 44 goals and 110 penalty minutes in the 1999–2000 season, crashing and banging his way to the top.

But Nolan is far from alone or secure as the game's premier power forward—on any night, tough, talented and always dangerous players like Brendan Shanahan, John LeClair, or Jason Arnott display their awesome brand of hockey.

Winston Churchill once said: "There is nothing to fear but fear itself."

In today's NHL, we can alter that a bit: "There is nothing to fear but a fearless player."

Jason ARNOTT

No matter what else Jason Arnott does in the rest of his hockey career, or even the rest of his life, he will be known forever for scoring the game-winning goal in overtime to give New Jersey the 2000 Stanley Cup.

The road to the Stanley Cup, however, was not paved with gold for Arnott. There were a lot of pot-holes along the way.

In his rookie season in Edmonton, it looked like it would be smooth driving, a one-way street to the top. Arnott jumped right into the NHL after being selected seventh overall in 1993 from the Oshawa Generals.

He didn't miss a turn, scoring 33 goals and 35 assists to finish a close second in the Calder Trophy balloting behind future teammate Martin Brodeur.

It was supposed to be the beginning of great things, but it turned out to be the beginning of the end. Some said instant success went to Arnott's head and he forgot the work ethic that got him there in the

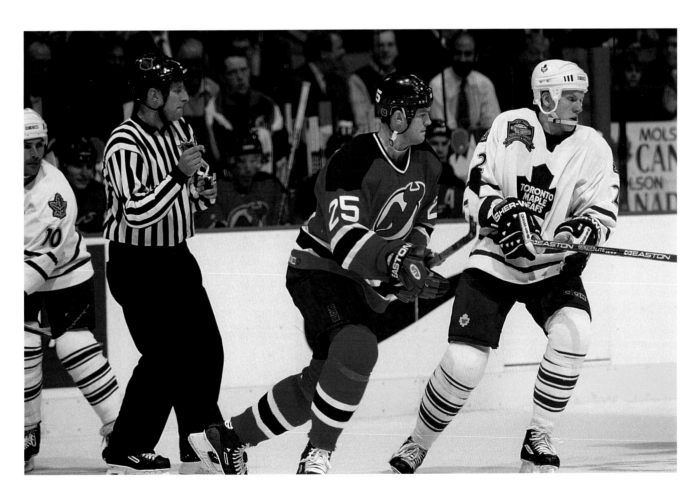

first place. Some said that expectations were set so high, he didn't have a hope of meeting them, and that it caused the media and fans to turn on him.

Arnott's offensive contribution dwindled each subsequent season, until he reached a low point in 1997–98, scoring just five goals in Edmonton's first 35 games. The pressure was too much—the pressure on himself to perform better, the pressure from the media, and the pressure from the fans.

Eventually, Edmonton General Manager Glen Sather determined that the only course of action was to trade Arnott. It would be best for the Oilers and best for Arnott. He was packaged in a deal that brought Bill Guerin from New Jersey. Guerin was an instant hit in Edmonton, while Arnott could manage just five goals the rest of the way, in 35 games. The New Jersey fans hardly figured they got the best of that deal, and the grumbling grew louder.

More pressure? Maybe, but it was different now. Arnott was maturing as both a person and a hockey player. Expectations were considerably lower, leaving him free to concentrate on hockey rather than the media circus that sometimes surrounds it in Canadian cities.

Slowly, he started to come around. He wasn't scoring 50 goals, and nobody thought he would, but he was making a contribution and becoming a more rounded player. The following season Arnott scored 27 goals and added 27 assists. The New Jersey style seemed to suit him better—it was more disciplined and the roles more defined.

During the 1999–2000 season, Arnott hooked up on a line with Petr Sykora and Patrik Elias. Arnott was the centerpiece, using his size and strength to create room for the skilled wingers, to battle along the boards for the puck, and to crash the net to get the

benefit of his linemates' slick playmaking. By the time the playoffs started, the three were very likely one of the top two or three lines in the league.

During the playoffs they were magic, and when all was said and done, Arnott was tied for third in the league in scoring, with eight goals and 12 assists in 23 games.

As he paraded the Stanley Cup around the ice and used a cell phone to call friends and family back home in Wasaga Beach, Ontario, the *Hockey Night in Canada* cameras repeatedly gravitated back to Arnott.

It had been just six years since his rookie season, but to Jason Arnott, it must have seemed like a lifetime.

Matthew BARNABY

The more people hate Matthew Barnaby, the happier it makes him. That's because it means he's doing his job.

Barnaby is an agitator, a scrapper, an annoying pest who runs around trying to bother people and throw them off their game, all the while infuriating them with his evil little grin. Everybody is a target, including opposing fans

In Philadelphia, where he may be hated the most, he's received death threats. All in a day's work, according to Barnaby, although he no longer answers his phone in that city.

Before games, during games, and after games, he's constantly gabbing at his opponents, trying to push their buttons and make them concentrate on him rather than the game. Even in the 2000 playoffs, during the pregame warm-up, he was yapping with Philadelphia backup John Vanbiesbrouck, pointing to the bench where he was suggesting Vanbiesbrouck would stay.

If Barnaby can draw a penalty and put his team on

the power play, he loves it, although he certainly spends more than his share of time in the penalty box himself. He's averaged 304 penalty minutes per 82 games over his career, with a season high of 335 for the Buffalo Sabres in 1995–96. Twice in junior hockey, he had more than 440 penalty minutes in a season. In his last year of junior, for Victoriaville in the Quebec League, he had 448 penalty minutes and 111 points, surely some kind of record.

His best NHL season statistically was in 1996–97, for Buffalo, when he scored 19 goals and added 24 assists. He wants to be a 20-goal scorer, which is pretty good in the NHL nowadays, even if you do nothing else.

That's the thing: Barnaby isn't just a goon, he can score and play the game. And when the playoffs come, he's even better. He led the Buffalo Sabres in scoring in the 1998 playoffs with seven goals and six assists in 15 games.

He's probably best known for scoring a hat trick on Mother's Day during the 1998 playoffs, with Buffalo, and then searching the crowd to find his mother.

Barnaby didn't have it easy growing up, and that may be where his toughness comes from. Raised by his mother, money was scarce, and sometimes they bought hockey sticks instead of food. He had to quit school for a while, at age 16, in order to earn enough money to pay his hockey fees.

One draft pick slot may have made the difference in his hockey career. When the Quebec League held its draft in 1990, he was the very last player chosen. It just made Barnaby more determined. He told the management of the Beauport team that once they saw him play there was no way they would be able to cut him. A couple seasons later he was a 100-point man and 400-penalty-minute earner.

A couple seasons after that, Barnaby was a regular in the NHL. He spent part of eight seasons with the Buffalo Sabres, and was adored by fans. When he was traded to Pittsburgh, he naturally became one of Buffalo's most despised enemies.

Sure, Matthew Barnaby is probably the most hated player in the league, but don't tell him that, because it'll just make him break out in that irritating gap-toothed grin. All in a day's work, as far as he's concerned.

Ed BELFOUR

Forget about Ed Belfour the hockey player for a minute, which isn't that easy to do, and consider Ed Belfour off the ice.

As if it's not enough stopping 100-mile-per-hour rubber disks for a living, he's got other dangerous pursuits. He has his scuba diving license, he flies planes, and he races cars.

In other words, Eddie the Eagle lives life in the fast lane. He's getting everything out of it that he can.

He's gotten everything out of his goaltending career, too. He's a model of inspiration for young players in terms of desire and perseverance. Belfour was actually cut from his high school hockey team, and he was never drafted by an NHL team.

That's strange for somebody who would go on to

become one of the best goalies in NHL history, during the regular season and playoffs.

Belfour opened a lot of eyes in his one and only year at North Dakota. He sported a 29-4 record and led them to the NCAA championship. That was enough for the Chicago Blackhawks to sign him to a contract and put him with their farm team in Saginaw, in the IHL. He shared rookie-of-the-year honors there, and was named to the first all-star team. He also started a trend that would carry over into his NHL career: he led the league in minutes played.

Belfour split his time between Saginaw and Chicago the next season. But then, still a rookie, he exploded onto the NHL scene, leading in games played, wins, minutes played, and goals against average. All that was good enough for a boatload of trophies, including the Calder as rookie of the year, the Vezina as best goalie, the Jennings for best goals against average, as well as a first-team all-star berth.

That was a start to what has been a great career. Belfour has led the NHL in shutouts four times, he's led in goals against average twice, and he's won the Vezina Trophy twice. He's the active shutout leader among all goalies, with 49, and has 308 career wins.

In the playoffs, Belfour has been even better. He's led in goals against average three times, and, of course, he won a Stanley Cup in 1999 with Dallas. He holds many records for both Chicago and Dallas, but one that stands out as an NHL record is 11 straight playoff wins in one season, with Chicago in 1992.

If you think Belfour is slowing down, think again. He was absolutely phenomenal during the 2000 playoffs. He probably wasn't far from winning the Conn

Smythe Trophy, either, a rare event for somebody from a losing team. His four shutouts tied an all-time record for one playoff year.

With Dallas on the ropes in the finals against New Jersey, Belfour played some of the best goal he or any netminder has ever played. In Game Five, he was unbelievable, holding the Devils off the scoreboard during regulation time and into the third overtime frame. Dallas finally won 1-0 when Mike Modano scored.

In Game Six, Belfour was at it again. He looked unbeatable, and it was only a perfect pass and perfect shot by Jason Arnott all alone in front of the net, during the second overtime, that gave New Jersey the 2-1 win and the Stanley Cup.

Nope, Ed Belfour isn't slowing down at all—on the ice or off it.

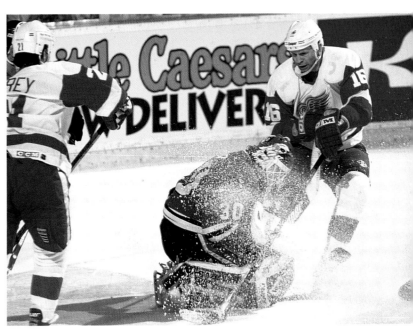

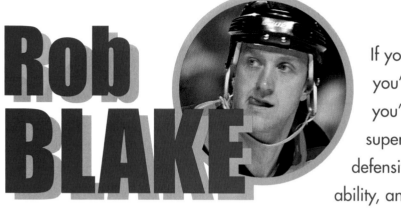

Rob BLAKE

If you were writing down all the things you'd want in an NHL defenseman, you'd probably list size, toughness, superior offensive ability, outstanding defensive ability, excellent power-play ability, and captain-like leadership skills.

To save time, you could just write down the name Rob Blake.

One thing you wouldn't put down on that piece of paper is injury-prone, which is the only complaint you can make about Blake. After being voted the Kings' most valuable defenseman in his first four years in the league, he played only 24 games the next season because of groin problems. The following year, he suffered a torn ACL in his knee and missed all but six games. The next year, he broke his hand; the year after that he won the Norris Trophy as the league's best defenseman; the year after that he broke his foot; and the year after that he was one of three finalists nominated for the Norris Trophy.

Whoa! Let's back up a bit to the 1997–98 season. The Norris Trophy wasn't a surprise, except that

Blake had been able to remain healthy enough to earn it. But that's what made it all the more impressive. Not only was he able to battle back from devastating injuries, he went one step further and asserted himself as the best defenseman in the league.

That pretty much says all you need to know about Rob Blake and why he is considered one of the most fearless players in the game.

The Los Angeles Kings captain isn't about to change his style of play just to avoid getting injured. He's big, at 6'4" and 224 pounds, and he uses his size for every aspect of the game, which is why he's one of the best in the NHL.

Blake can turn a game around with a booming bodycheck or a booming slapshot. Twice he's had at least 20 goals in a season, and were it not for the injuries, he'd be around that total every season.

The power play is where Blake's offensive skills

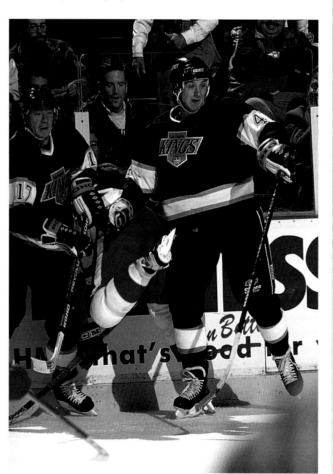

are most evident. Of his 121 career goals, 67 came with the man advantage.

The Simcoe, Ontario, native has built up quite an international résumé. Blake played in the 1998 Olympics, where he was named the tournament's top defenseman. The year before he also was named top defenseman and helped Canada win the gold medal at the world championships. He also played for Canada in 1991, 1994 (gold medal), 1996, 1998 (world championships), and 1999.

The captain of the Los Angeles Kings was at it again in the 1999–2000 season. Blake was the third-top scoring defenseman, with stats of 18-39-57, second in the league, with 327 shots, and one of the three finalists for the Norris Trophy.

You could say that injuries have held Rob Blake back from winning more awards and having an even more successful career. But you could also say that injuries have made him an even better player.

Chris CHELIOS

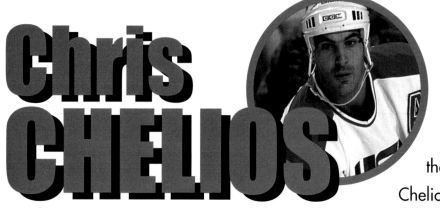

If NHL forwards were voting on their least fun thing to do during a hockey game, it just might be standing in front of the opponent's net when Chris Chelios is playing defense.

Chelios will do absolutely anything to move you out of there, anything to stop you from scoring on his team, and anything to win. It doesn't matter if it's allowed in the rule book or not. And often it isn't.

Although it doesn't seem quite right to see Chelios playing in a Detroit uniform after being with the Chicago Blackhawks for nine years, Montreal Canadiens fans can still picture him in their uniform, where he started his career and played seven seasons.

He joined Montreal after playing with the United States Olympic team in 1984. Prior to that, he was at the University of Wisconsin for two years.

The trade that sent Chelios from Montreal to Chicago for Denis Savard isn't one Canadiens fans brag

about. Savard had a few decent seasons at the end of his career, but was hardly comparable at that point to Chelios.

Sometimes, though, players can get stale in a city and a new start can give them new life. Obviously, it worked for Chelios, who went back to his hometown and excelled for nine seasons.

Chelios isn't a kid anymore, but still plays like it. That's why, at age 38 and in his 17th NHL season, there was Chelios, second in the league in plus-minus, with a +48.

Chelios has that rare ability among NHL defense-men to combine offensive skill, defensive excellence, and physical intimidation. He's won the Norris Trophy three times, has been a first-team all-star five times, and has scored over 50 points eight times. Six times, he's had over 60 points, and he's reached the 70 plateau twice, once with Montreal and once with Chicago.

He's had over 100 minutes in penalties twelve times, four of those over 200 minutes, including 282 in the 1992–93 season, the same year he won a Norris Trophy. That many penalty minutes is the most ever for a Norris Trophy winner, which tells you something about the way Chelios plays.

Only three defensemen have more penalty minutes than Chelios's 2,385: Marty McSorley, Dave Manson, and Scott Stevens. Chelios doesn't fight a lot. Even when he had 282 penalty minutes, he only had four majors. Don't let that fool you, though; not many players during his career have gotten the better of him. He did, however, have 10 misconducts that season.

Chelios passed legendary defensemen Bobby Orr and Borje Salming on the all-time assist list during the 1999–2000 season, and sits with 664. Only Paul Coffey, Ray Bourque, Larry Murphy, Al MacInnis, Phil Housley, and Brad Park have more among defensemen.

What this means, simply enough, is that Chelios is one of the best all-around defensemen in the history of the NHL.

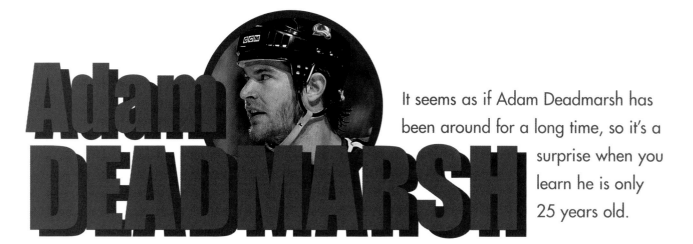

Adam DEADMARSH

It seems as if Adam Deadmarsh has been around for a long time, so it's a surprise when you learn he is only 25 years old.

Already, he's played over 400 games in six NHL regular seasons, as well as 88 playoff games. And he has his name engraved on the Stanley Cup.

Actually, he's had two names etched in the Cup. The first time, they spelled his name incorrectly, "Deadmarch" instead of Deadmarsh. They did fix it,

The Colorado Avalanche already have more than their share of skilled stars. They've got Peter Forsberg, Joe Sakic, Sandis Ozolinsh, Patrick Roy, Ray Bourque, and a couple young stars in Milan Hejduk and Chris Drury. Those players have the ability to make others around them better. Sometimes, it doesn't even matter who they play with. Deadmarsh, however, has the rare ability to make the stars shine brighter, and they want him playing on their line.

As a smallish power forward by NHL standards— 6'0", 195 pounds— Deadmarsh plays a lot bigger. He's strong, aggressive, and determined. Many nights he'll lead the team in hits, and in every game he creates room for the more skilled players. As an added bonus, he can put the puck in the net or on the stick of a teammate. When someone else has the puck, he feels it's his job to drive to the net, which he does as well as any player in the league.

however, making Adam the only player in NHL history to have his name corrected on the Stanley Cup.

That's hardly his only claim to fame, however, and neither are the Deadmarsh Deli Dills or Deadmarsh Pickled Pucks that you can pick up at your local Denver grocer. Despite leading the Avalanche in goal scoring, with 33 in 1996–97 (his career high), Deadmarsh rarely plays a starring role. He's more of a support player—mind you, a top-of-the-linesupport player. If the NHL were the Academy Awards, he'd be up for Best Player in a Supporting Role on a yearly basis.

That's why Deadmarsh is so effective alongside somebody like Peter Forsberg, whose talents aren't wasted trying to carry an inferior player along with him. That was evident in the 2000 playoffs, when Deadmarsh and Forsberg tied for the team lead in scoring, with 15 points each.

You get the impression that someday Deadmarsh could be a 40-goal scorer, although he seems to have established his annual assist total at 27. In a statistical oddity, he's had exactly that number in four of his five full-season campaigns.

But Deadmarsh's goal isn't to be the top goal scorer on the team; it's to help somebody else do that, and more importantly, to help his team win.

Shane DOAN

Shane Doan likes to get high. High in the air, that is, where he's learning to fly, and even a cloud or two above that when he talks about his Christian beliefs.

When he wants to get down, it's on the ice, where he had a career year with the Phoenix Coyotes in the 1999–2000 season, finishing second on the team in scoring. The big power forward jumped from six goals and 16 assists to 26 goals and 25 assists in his fourth NHL season.

It hasn't been an easy rise for Doan. Getting to the top always meant overcoming barriers. After growing up on a Christian ranch in Halkirk, Alberta, his lifestyle choice was severely tested when he left home at 16, moving 600 miles away to play junior hockey in Kamloops, British Columbia. He made a conscious decision to fight the temptations that can lead teenagers down the wrong roads. While he admits he's not perfect, Doan couldn't have won the war without fighting those battles.

Doan played three seasons in Kamloops, leading the team to the Memorial Cup in 1995, and earning the Most Valuable Player award in the process.

He became a highly sought-after draft choice that summer. Teams liked his size, his dedication, his leadership abilities, his strength, and his character. When Winnipeg's turn came to select with the seventh overall pick, they snapped Doan up, much to the chagrin of the Montreal Canadiens, who had the next pick and desperately wanted him.

Doan jumped right to the Jets from junior and earned an assist in his first NHL game. But the points weren't going to come that easy for a few years. He scored just seven his first year, followed by four the next, when the team moved to Phoenix. Then he had just five in 1996–97, when he also had his first taste of the minors, scoring 21 goals and 21 assists for the Phoenix farm team in Springfield.

Back in the NHL full time, the struggles continued. Doan scored just six goals. He admits he was getting worried, but he never gave up faith in himself, or faith in his Christian beliefs. Doan's steadfastness finally paid off in the 1999–2000 season, when he had his breakout year.

"The difference for me is that I have a bottom line to return to, a sure foundation that I can stand on that will not shift or change or crumble beneath me: The Word of God—nothing more, nothing less, nothing else."

Sometimes an athlete with Christian beliefs can be the object of ridicule, but Shane Doan isn't afraid of what people think. In fact, he's not afraid of anything, whether it's in the air, on the ground, or on the ice.

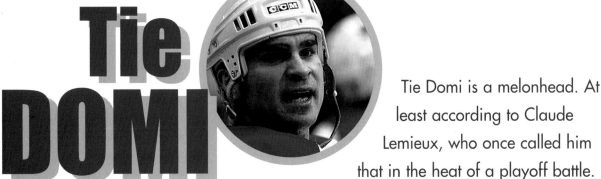

Tie DOMI

Tie Domi is a melonhead. At least according to Claude Lemieux, who once called him that in the heat of a playoff battle.

But the popular Toronto Maple Leaf with the smooth-shaved head has been called a lot worse names and will continue to be as long as he remains one of the NHL's premier tough guys.

Most of the enforcers in the NHL are much bigger than Domi, who is listed as standing only 5 feet 10 inches tall. He starts the majority of his fights looking up, and finishes the majority of them looking down.

That pitbull mentality has made Domi one of the most popular Toronto athletes. As the saying goes, it's

not the amount of dog in the fight, it's the amount of fight in the dog.

Domi gained the single-season penalty mark with the Maple Leafs when he earned 365 in the 1997–98 season. He also holds the Phoenix franchise record, with 347 in the 1993–94 season, when the team was still in Winnipeg. Three times he's had over 300 penalty minutes in one season, and three other times he's had over 200. Twice he had 198. Heading into the 2000–2001 season, he had earned 2,656 penalty minutes, the equivalent of just over 44 complete games. He should soon move into the top 10 of all-time.

That cuts a deep slice out of his ice time, but Domi knows why he is in the NHL, and knows how to stay

there, although he was also very upset when he was benched in the 1998–1999 playoffs by Toronto coach Pat Quinn. Tough guys still have to be able to play the game, was the message directed at Domi. And in the play-offs, fighting is rare.

Domi was always a good skater, but he set his mind and body to getting into the best shape possible for the 1999–2000

season. Sitting in the press box was not something he wanted to do again.

In the 2000 playoffs he was in the lineup for all 12 of Toronto's playoff games. That was a compliment in itself, but when a teammate went down with injuries, Quinn moved Domi up to the third line, another big compliment.

Don't get confused, though, because Domi doesn't. He knows where his value to the Maple Leafs lies, and that's in stirring up the opposition any way he knows how. If he can score a goal in the process, all the better. His career high is 11.

During the 2000 playoffs, Domi had words with Andre Roy, of the Ottawa Senators. When Roy didn't accept the challenge, Domi flapped his arms like a chicken. Roy responded by getting down on his knees, as if to lower himself to Domi's height, and throwing fake punches.

Roy knew it wouldn't be that easy, however. Tie Domi may be small, but if you underestimate him, you'll soon be overmatched.

Theoren FLEURY

Theoren Fleury's favorite hockey player when he was growing up was Stan Mikita of the Chicago Blackhawks.

Mikita was partially deaf, and had to overcome that handicap to be successful in the NHL.

Funny thing about that—Fleury has a hearing impairment as well. Oh, he can hear okay; he just doesn't *listen*. If he did, he never would have played a game in the NHL. Fleury is only five feet six inches tall, and anybody who knows anything about hockey knows that's too small to play in the best hockey league in the world.

If Fleury had believed that for a second, he wouldn't have managed any of these accomplishments:

★ Led the WHL junior league in scoring, with 160 points in 1987–88.

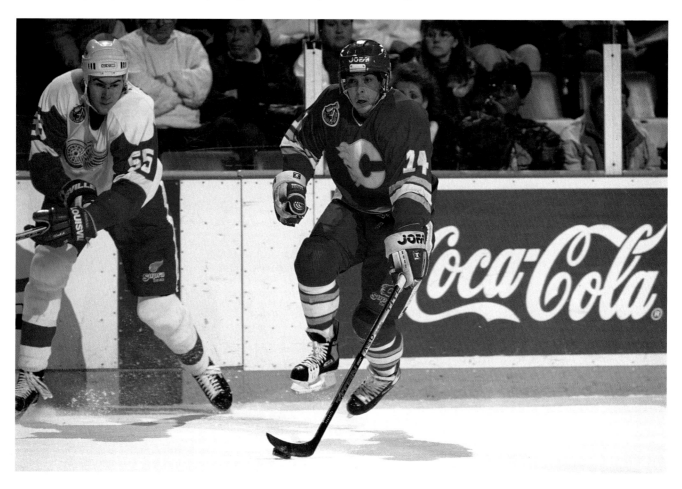

★ Won a gold medal at the world junior hockey championships as captain of Canada's team.

★ Played in the NHL only a year after being drafted 166th overall in the eighth round of the entry draft in 1987.

★ Won a Stanley Cup in his first NHL season.

★ Became the Calgary Flames all-time leader in goals and points.

★ Played in the all-star game six times.

★ Played for Team Canada at the 1988 Olympics, five times internationally as a pro, and seven times total.

★ Won a Canada Cup and two silver medals in world competition.

★ Scored at least 100 points twice, and over 90 points twice.

★ Earned 197 penalty minutes in one season, and 186 in another, and has a career total of 1,421.

★ Scored at least 40 goals four times, including a 51-goal season in 1990–91.

★ Tied for the best plus-minus in 1990–91, with a +48.

★ Has eight seasons of playing at least 80 games.

★ Has earned over 500 assists and 900 points in the NHL.

Fleury isn't even close to being finished. By the time he's through, he will have over 400 goals and 1,000 points.

Growing up in Russell, Manitoba, Fleury didn't stray from Western Canada for most of his hockey career. He played junior in Moose Jaw, Saskatchewan, and then spent the first 11 years of his NHL career in Calgary, Alberta.

With unrestricted free agency looming, and the economic climate of the NHL being what it is, Fleury was dealt to the Colorado Avalanche during the 1998–99 season to help with their playoff run. He certainly did his part, scoring 24 points in 15 regular-season games, and 20 more in 18 playoff contests.

When the season was over, Fleury signed as a free agent with the New York Rangers. Moving to the Big Apple was an

adjustment for the small-town boy from Western Canada, and his initial season there was not a particularly good one. Turmoil constantly surrounded the team, they weren't winning, and Fleury had only 15 goals—the fewest in his career for a full season. He did, however, finish second on the team, with 64 points.

As if Fleury hasn't had enough obstacles in his path, he was recently diagnosed with Crohn's Disease, which requires constant treatment. Just one more thing he has to deal with and find a way to overcome. When you think about it, we shouldn't even know Theoren Fleury's name, much less recognize him as one of the most inspirational and fearless players in NHL history.

Peter FORSBERG

Who is the best player in the NHL today? Good arguments could be made for Jaromir Jagr and Peter Forsberg, with a couple others thrown into the mix for good measure.

But if you want to talk about the most *complete* player in the NHL, there's no debate: It's Forsberg, hands down.

Forsberg can score goals and is one of the best playmakers in the game. He plays defense, he's intense, he can check, he can hit, and he's got a mean streak in him.

Doesn't sound like a Swede, does it, which is sort of

a backhanded compliment. Forsberg would break the mold no matter which country he was from.

Forsberg was originally drafted by the Philadelphia Flyers, sixth overall in 1991. He didn't come over to North America until he was ready, which was three years later. In the meantime, he had become part of one

of the most celebrated trades in NHL history. When Eric Lindros refused to report to Quebec, Forsberg was included in a package deal that included Chris Simon, Ron Hextall, Mike Ricci, Steve Duchesne, and two first rounders.

Ironically, right now there's probably no player in the league the Avalanche would consider trading for Forsberg, including Lindros.

Forsberg only spent one year in Quebec before they moved to Colorado, but he didn't waste any time showing his stuff. He won the Calder Trophy as rookie of the year, when he earned 50 points in 47 games, in the labor-shortened season of 1994–95.

It just got better after that. He had 116 points in his sophomore season and won the Stanley Cup. The year after that, he was runner-up as best defensive forward in the Selke Trophy voting. Then he was a first-team all-star for two seasons in a row, and led all playoff scorers, with 24 points in 1999.

Off-season shoulder surgery meant Forsberg missed most of the first half of the 1999–2000 season, but he wasted no time getting back into the swing of things. In his first game back he had five points, two goals, and three assists. By the playoffs, he was like his old self, finishing tied for eighth in scoring, with 15 points in 17 games.

Forsberg has made quite a name for himself internationally as well. Canadian fans will remember him scoring the winning goal in a shootout, to give Sweden the gold medal at the Olympics in 1994. He also was a member of the 1992 World Cup winning team, and twice won silver medals with the junior national team.

Forsberg no doubt also has a spot reserved for him in the NHL record books, and eventually the Hockey Hall of Fame.

When all is said and done, not only will Peter Forsberg be recognized as one of the best Swedes to play the game, but one of the best to play the game, period.

Bill GUERIN

Bill Guerin is a pain in the butt. Both on the ice and off.

Off the ice, he's had celebrated contract disputes and holdouts, and has demanded trades from New Jersey and Edmonton. Mind you, those are two of the more frugal organizations in the league.

On the ice, the fifth overall selection in the 1989 draft by New Jersey looks like a 50-goal scorer, but doesn't have the stats to back it up. He's a good scorer, not a great scorer. He's had just one 30-goal season, for

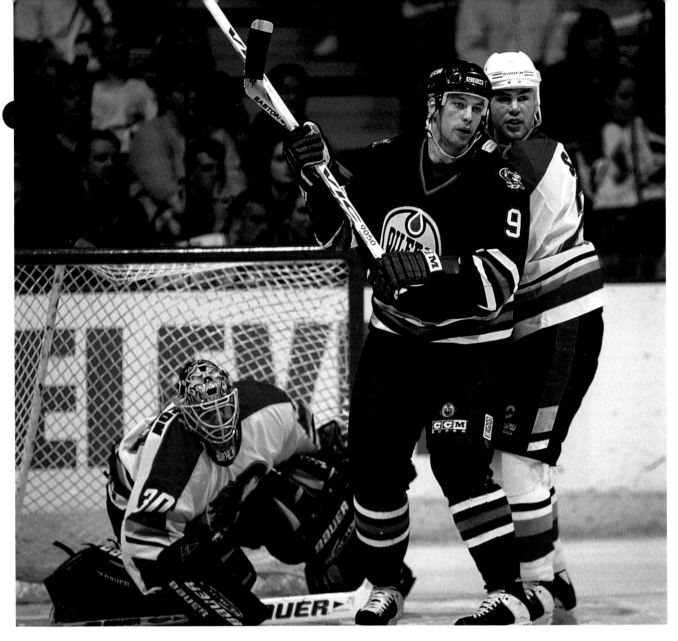

Edmonton in 1998–99, when he was selected as the team's most valuable player. He's had five seasons in the twenties.

So what does Guerin bring to the table?

He's one of the relatively new breed of tough American players, along with the likes of Keith Tkachuk and Jeremy Roenick, whom every center in the league wishes was on his wing. American center Doug Weight certainly can breathe and score more easily, knowing Guerin is patrolling the right side for the Edmonton Oilers.

Guerin is an intimidating presence on the ice. That presence creates more room for others, thereby making his value far greater than the sum of his goals and assists. On top of that, he's an outstanding skater and uses that strength to blow by an opponent, as readily as he can smash an opposing player into the boards and take the puck away from him.

That's not to say Guerin doesn't have value as a goal scorer and playmaker, along with being a physical force. Scoring 20 goals and earning over 100 PIM isn't an easy thing to do in the NHL. Only ten players were able to do that in the 1999–2000 season. The year before, when he had 30 goals and over 100 penalty minutes, just four other players also managed it. Only Guerin and Brendan Shanahan are on both lists.

Guerin has managed 20 goals and over 100 PIM four times in his career, just missing on a couple other occasions. He's a streaky scorer, but when he gets on a roll it appears as if nothing can stop him. If he can manage to keep it going for an entire season, and he's in the right situation, he's a candidate for 40 goals.

Dominik HASEK

It's hard to believe that the man many believe is one of the best goaltenders in NHL history was once a 27-year-old backup, shuffling between the NHL and IHL.

But that's exactly what Dominik Hasek was in Chicago, in his first two seasons in North America, spelling Ed Belfour once in a while.

Hasek was selected 207th overall in the 1983 draft, but chose not to come to North America until 1990, when he was already 25 years old. This was after being selected as the Czechoslovakian goal-tender of the year for the five previous seasons.

There was no room in the Chicago net, of course, with Belfour winning the Vezina Trophy in 1990, and playing a league-high 74 games. So, you couldn't blame the general manager at the time, Mike Keenan, for pulling the trigger on what would turn out to be one of the most lopsided trades in league history.

Hasek would never have played much in Chicago.

Buffalo gave up another goaltender, Stephane Beauregard, and a fourth-round draft pick, and got what they thought was a backup to another great goaltender, Grant Fuhr.

Hasek's first season in Buffalo was largely undistinguished, but his second season was magic. He led the league with a 1.95 goals against average and seven shutouts. At 29, a superstar was born.

After that, it just got ridiculous. Hasek won the Vezina Trophy that season, and in five of the next six seasons overall. He won the Hart Trophy twice as the league's most valuable player, and was a first-team all-star five times.

Along the way, he picked up the nickname The Dominator, and was acknowl-

edged by virtually everyone to be the best goaltender on the planet.

Hasek is not what you would call an orthodox goalie by any stretch of the imagination. They don't teach his style in any goaltending schools. He has just one goal—to stop goals—and any way he can do it, that's what he's going to do. He flips, he flops, he throws down his goalie stick and dives across the net. Anything at all. He has amazing reflexes, and just as it looks as if the puck is going to enter the net, his leg kicks out of nowhere and stops it.

Even more impressive, Hasek was not playing on particularly good Sabres teams. If they won, it was usually because of him. He was the only goalie for years who was the sole determining factor of whether or not his team won. He was outshot most every night, and his save percentage was astounding. In fact, he was the league leader, or tied, for seven straight seasons.

The one thing Hasek hasn't won is a Stanley Cup, although he came very close in the 1999 playoffs, taking the Sabres to the finals by posting 1.77 goals against average. They beat out Ottawa, Boston and Toronto to win the Eastern Conference, and then faced Dallas in the finals, losing in Game Six on that highly disputed goal by Brett Hull.

The 1999–2000 season was to be Hasek's last, but he missed much of the year with injuries, so he'll play one more season. Or, to put it another way, he'll *dominate* for one more season.

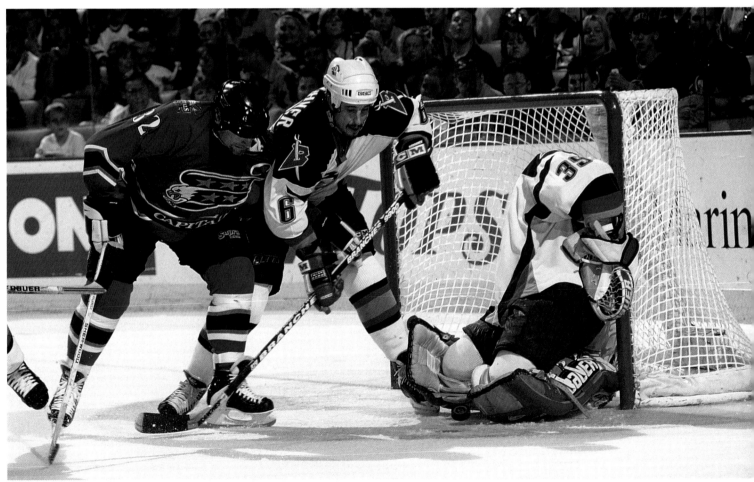

Derian HATCHER

Either Derian Hatcher is getting more notice or he's getting better. Whatever it is, this guy is one of the best defensemen in the National Hockey League.

To start with, Hatcher is a one-man wrecking crew on the ice. He uses every inch and every pound of his 6′5″, 225-pound frame to make opponents wish they had taken up careers in badminton rather than hockey.

He doesn't just hit opponents, he flattens them, punishes them, crunches them, puts them through the boards. He's in a league with a select few that includes Scott Stevens and Chris Pronger, defensemen

who can turn the tide of a game with a devastating hit or five.

Something else these three have in common is that they're so good at hitting clean, they don't need to be dirty. And they don't need to worry much about retribution because few players are likely to get the best of them, or even a part of them.

Mind you, Hatcher does let his emotions get the better of him at times; occasionally he will take a bad penalty or not play completely by the rules. Ask Jason Arnott, who lost five teeth courtesy of Hatcher

during the 2000 finals. Or maybe you could ask Jeremy Roenick, who suffered a broken jaw at the expense of Hatcher in the 1999 playoffs, resulting in a seven-game suspension, the second longest in playoff history. Or maybe you could even ask Pronger, who was the recipient of a Hatcher cross-check, for which Hatcher was suspended for four games.

But if you're going to stand around in front of the Dallas net when Hatcher is on the ice, you'd better be prepared to at least lose some teeth. Many opposing forwards opt not to get too close.

Defensively, the Dallas captain is also one of the best in the game. He and partner Richard Matvichuk are always on the ice against the opposing team's best line. In fact, it seems the two of them are always on the ice, period.

Hatcher isn't the offensive force his brother Kevin was in his prime, when he had a couple seasons in the 70-point range for the Washington Capitals, but he's not going to hurt you either. He can play on the power play if needed, and has a good shot. He also knows just when to join the rush, as he did in the three-overtime Game Five of the 2000 finals, just missing the corner of the net with a good chance.

Both Derian and his brother played their junior careers in North Bay, Ontario and both were drafted in the first round. Derian was selected eighth overall by the Minnesota North Stars in 1999. Kevin went 17th over-all to Washington in 1984. The Michigan natives played together for two years in Dallas, in 1994–95 and 1995–96.

The Dallas Stars captain has one Stanley Cup to his credit, in 1999, and there may be more in the future. Another trophy Derian Hatcher may soon win is the Norris Trophy, as the league's best defenseman.

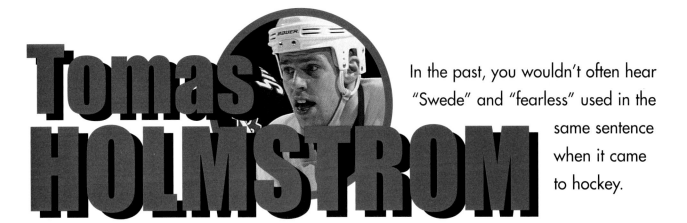

Tomas HOLMSTROM

In the past, you wouldn't often hear "Swede" and "fearless" used in the same sentence when it came to hockey.

It used to be Dino Ciccarelli who was best known for standing in front of the net, screening and pestering opposing goaltenders. Now it's Tomas Holmstrom.

Holmstrom takes a licking—a severe pounding is more like it—and keeps on ticking. Every single game, he parks himself in front of the goal crease and takes whatever big opposing defensemen and irritated goalies can dish out.

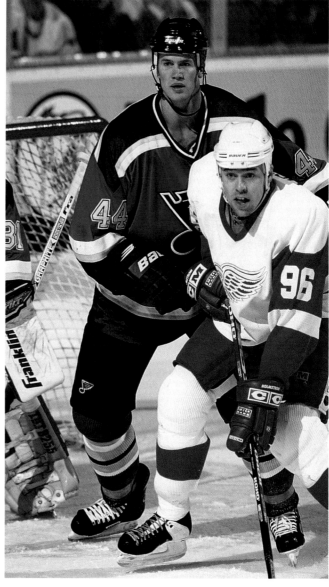

He's trying to screen the netminder or tip in a shot from the point. He's trying to throw his opponents off their game, forcing them to focus on him and perhaps draw a penalty to give his team an advantage: anything to help the team win. That unselfishness cuts into Holmstrom's personal statistics, but doesn't diminish his value. His teammates and opponents know how effective he is.

Holmstrom probably gets more assists that don't get into the scoring stats than any player in the league. After his first four seasons, his goal high is only 13 and his point high is 35. In his only two full seasons, he earned 34 and then 35. But he has two of something that most players don't even have one of— Stanley Cup rings.

In the first Detroit Cup win, in 1997, Holmstrom only played one game, but the following year, in the second win, he was instrumental in the team's victory, exposing yet another of his talents. Holmstrom comes to play when it counts the most.

In the 1998 Stanley Cup run, he was third in scoring, only five points behind teammate Steve

Yzerman and only one behind Sergei Fedorov. In 1999, he had seven points in ten games, and in 2000 was considered by the Detroit media to be the best Red Wing forward in the playoffs.

These are pretty heady accomplishments for a player who was 11th in scoring on the Wings during the 1999–2000 regular season and 11th the season before.

But we know Holmstrom's value is far greater than the sum of his statistics. He also knows how to play it smart. He doesn't take a lot of penalty minutes. When he parks himself in front of the net, the most natural thing in the world would be to retaliate for the beatings he takes. But he doesn't. Tomas Holmstrom takes it all, then he takes some more. And then he'll grin his toothless grin, which just infuriates his opponents even more.

A chicken Swede? Not this guy.

Jaromir JAGR

Some players intimidate with their shot, some with their size, some with their speed, and still others with their toughness.

Jaromir Jagr intimidates just by stepping on the ice. He's not feared for his rough play, or his stick-work, or his attitude. He's feared because he can make any opposing player on the ice look as if he took up the wrong sport.

Jagr has all the tools to be the best player in the NHL, and he uses them, which is why he is the best player in the NHL. He is big, at 6'2", 230 pounds; he's strong, especially on his skates, where it's nearly impossible to knock him off the puck; he has a hard, accurate

shot; he has some of the quickest, smoothest moves with the puck ever seen in the NHL; he has great vision of the whole ice surface, which makes him an excellent passer; and he has breakaway speed, which he uses whenever he needs it.

The Czech caused quite a stir when he was named the 38th-best player in NHL history by *The Hockey News*, in 1998. He hadn't played long enough, some said. He's not that good, said others.

When all is said and done, he may not have been rated high enough. He seems destined for the top 10 at the very least, and top five isn't out of the question.

In 1999–2000, he won his third consecutive Art Ross Trophy, as the league's top scorer, and his fourth overall. This despite playing only 63 games. He's won four scoring championships overall, and came in second once, in 1995–96, despite recording the highest point total in NHL history by a right winger (149) and the most assists (87). Ironically, the scoring leader that season was teammate Mario Lemieux.

Earlier in his career, Jagr seemed to be caught

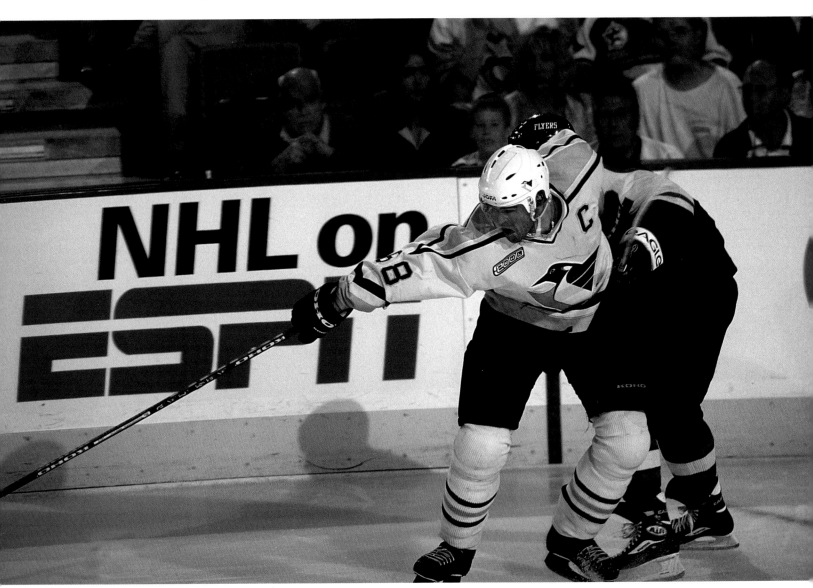

behind Lemieux's shadow. There was that inescapable question of whether or not Jagr was effective just because of his legendary teammate. Lemieux had the ability to make everyone around him a better player, and, of course, to help their scoring stats tremendously.

Jagr dispelled those notions for good, winning the scoring championship in the labor-shortened 1995–96 season, a year Lemieux took off to help his ailing back.

As it turned out, Jagr and Lemieux are remarkably similar on-ice talents. It doesn't matter who are the other members of their line, each dominates a game they are playing in, and each makes everybody else on the ice with them appear to be that much better.

Only a few players every generation come along like that, and if not for recurring groin problems, Jagr would have been even more dominant.

He's been a first-team all-star five times, has won the Pearson Trophy for MVP as voted on by the players, has a Hart Trophy as the league's MVP, and just missed a second one in the closest vote in NHL history, in 1999–2000, losing to Chris Pronger by a single point.

The scary thing about all of this, at least for those who play against him, is that Jaromir Jagr probably hasn't even reached his prime.

Curtis JOSEPH

Curtis Joseph had a mediocre game. That fact was newsworthy in itself, with the next day's headlines suggesting that he may, after all, be "human."

That's how good Joseph is. Most of the time he plays as if he's out of this world.

Only two goaltenders in recent years have been almost solely responsible for their team's success. One is Dominik Hasek, and the other, of course, is Joseph.

Goalies are often the product of their team—if the team is good, so are they; if the team is weak, they are,

too. With Hasek, his contribution can be proven statistically, because he's annually the leader in save percentage. But with Joseph, you just have to watch him. Or at least watch the highlights on the nightly sportscasts.

You'd have a hard time coming up with the right word to describe his play. Incredible, amazing, fantastic, awesome, unbelievable—any of those would do,

or any synonyms to that effect.

The Toronto Maple Leafs have not been a particularly strong team in recent seasons, especially on defense. That's what makes their 1999–2000 season so impressive, earning 100 points for the first time in their history.

There isn't a player on that team, however, who wouldn't tell you that without Joseph, the Leafs wouldn't have gotten that many points. In fact, making the playoffs without him would have been very unlikely.

A great oddity about Joseph is that he was never drafted into the NHL. He went to the University of Wisconsin in 1988–89, where it took NHL scouts one season to start their drooling. St. Louis signed him as a free agent at the end of that season, and the next year he was playing in the NHL.

He had six winning seasons in St. Louis before being dealt to Edmonton, where he awed the Oilers faithful fans, especially during the playoffs, in which the team pulled off some amazing first-round upsets over Colorado and Dallas. Most of the credit was handed directly to Joseph.

Unfortunately for Edmonton fans, the team was not able to afford one of the best goalies in the NHL, and Toronto signed Joseph as a free agent.

He's taken the city by storm and is easily the most popular athlete in the city. It wouldn't be a stretch to suggest that Joseph is one of the most popular athletes in the sporting history of the city.

Joseph is mindful of his community responsibilities as one of the city's heroes. He has "Cujo's Kids," a program in which 16 kids from local hospitals get to go to a Leafs game, sit in a private box, and, if there's time, meet Curtis Joseph after the game.

Curtis Joseph was honored for his charitable contributions at the 2000 NHL awards when he was presented with the King Clancy Memorial Trophy.

Darius KASPARAITIS

Darius Kasparaitis had better be fearless. Otherwise, he probably couldn't be an effective player in the NHL.

He's a wanted man, considered by many to be the dirtiest player in the league.

He was a wanted man back in the 1992 NHL draft as well, with the New York Islanders making a deal with Toronto so that they could draft him fifth over-all. It turned out to be a smart move.

The Lithuanian-born player is small by NHL defensemen standards, at just 5'11", but he's solid. When he hits players, Kasparaitis sometimes hits them low and they end up with injuries, often to their knees.

But when players hit as hard as Kasparaitis does, there's always the chance of an injury. It doesn't have to be a dirty hit. Kasparaitis is considered by many to be

the best open-ice hitting defenseman in the National Hockey League. Were it not for his reputation, you might have seen him on an all-star team or two.

You could ask Eric Lindros about that. In 1998, Kasparaitis knocked him out cold with a devastating clean hit with his shoulder, catching Lindros with his head down. Lindros was diagnosed subsequently with a grade-two concussion.

You might ask J.P. Dumont about the hits that aren't so clean. Kasparaitis was handed a two-game suspension by the NHL for what was termed a deliberate elbow to the head against a player not in possession of the puck or in a position to defend himself. The Blackhawks, Dumont's team at the time, vowed retribution against Kasparaitis when they met again.

Kasparaitis just shrugs off those kinds of threats. He's heard them before, lots of times. He knows players and fans hate him, and in a way it helps him to be a better player. In fact, he likes going into places where he's hated. It pumps up the intensity and can give his team an edge.

Kasparaitis is not going to break any scoring records. He looks after his own end, first and foremost. His career goal high for a season is just four, and his point high was 21, in his rookie year.

His rookie year and the next three seasons were spent with the Islanders, before he was traded to Pittsburgh, who badly needed some toughness on the blueline. They got that, and plenty more.

Most of the teams in the league are not very fond of Darius Kasparaitis, but most would also prefer to have him in their own lineup.

Martin LAPOINTE

You don't hear a lot about Martin Lapointe during the regular season. That's because he saves his headlines for the playoffs, somewhat reminiscent of another French Canadian, Claude Lemieux.

Even during games, you might not notice him until the team needs a big hit or a big goal. Then suddenly, there's Lapointe, and the momentum of the game is changed instantly.

Lapointe came out of the Quebec Junior League touted as a big-time scorer. In his last season there, he had 89 points in just 35 games. In the playoffs he was the league leader in goals, assists, and points, starting his reputation as a big-game player.

The Red Wings selected the right winger 10th

overall in the first round in 1991. He was up and down between Adirondack and Detroit in his first few years as a pro. The goals and points came in the minors, but not in the NHL.

Lapointe understood that in order to stay in the NHL, he had to develop another part of his game. He became proficient at the defensive part, while maintaining a crash-and-bang attitude on offense.

That doesn't translate into big offensive numbers, but it hasn't mattered because of the other qualities Lapointe brings to the table. Over the past four years he's had one season of 15 goals and three of 16 goals, while averaging around 140 penalty minutes.

The playoffs are a special time of year for

Lapointe, and it shows. He was a key performer in two Detroit Stanley Cup wins, doing anything he could to score, or to keep the other team from scoring. It's the time of year when everybody on the opposing team hates his guts. That's fine with him; he's not on the ice to make friends, he's out there to win. In Detroit's 1998 Cup triumph, he had nine goals in 21 games, including the Stanley Cup–winning goal. This tells you something about Lapointe's desire to win when it counts most. A 16-goal scorer suddenly becomes the second-top goal scorer in the playoffs, only one short of teammate Steve Yzerman.

This past season, Lapointe notched his first playoff hat-trick. Two of those goals came on the power play, surpassing his one power play goal scored in the entire regular season.

Lapointe has just one fault, if you can call it that: He tends to get too caught up emotionally in the game, which at times can lead to dumb penalties. He has to learn not to retaliate and to pick his spots, like his teammate Tomas Holmstrom does.

Martin Lapointe isn't going to lead the NHL in regular season scoring any time soon, but in the playoffs you can count on him to lead his team to victory for many years to come.

John LeCLAIR

John LeClair isn't your typical power forward. He doesn't get many penalties, doesn't fight, isn't one to do trash-talking on the ice or in the media, and doesn't do a lot of crashing around in front of the net or in the corners. But don't get the idea that he's some kind of big wimp.

He is big, at 6′3″, 226 pounds, and he uses that size effectively to create space for himself, especially around the net. It's almost as if there's radar connecting his eyes with the twine. Once he locks into his target, nothing can stop him from getting the puck there.

Certainly, he has the stats to prove it. From the start of the 1995–96 season through the 1999–2000 season, nobody in the NHL has scored more than the 235 goals he's slammed home.

Speaking of home, LeClair comes from St. Albans, Vermont, population: 12,000; NHL population: one. He's a hometown boy at heart, and made quite a splash when he brought the Stanley Cup to town after winning it with Montreal in 1993.

LeClair attended the University of Vermont, where he was drafted in the second round of the 1987 draft, by the Montreal Canadiens.

He only spent eight games in the minors before

son, LeClair was involved in a blockbuster trade with Philadelphia. He, along with the Flyers' future captain Eric Desjardins and Gilbert Dionne, was dealt for Mark Recchi and a third-round draft choice. Oddly enough, several years later, Recchi would be traded back to Philadelphia, giving that team all three principals of the trade.

Upon his arrival in the City of Brotherly Love, LeClair was instantly placed on the left wing of Eric

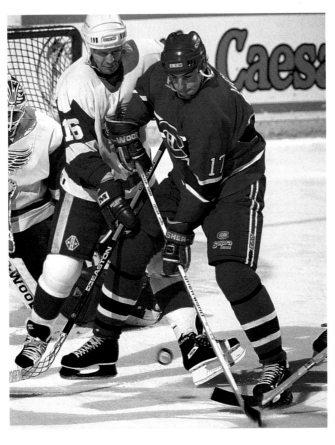

earning a permanent spot with the Canadiens at left wing. He helped the team win the Stanley Cup in 1993, but his four years in Montreal were otherwise undistinguished. His goal high was just 19, which isn't out of the ordinary for a player breaking into the league in his first few seasons.

In Montreal, however, which is just 70 miles from St. Albans, it constitutes a disappointment. With just one goal in his first nine games in the 1994–95 sea-

Lindros. It was a match made in heaven. In 37 games that first season, he scored 25 goals. And he was just getting started.

He had 50-goal seasons in each of the next three years, an accomplishment made more notable by the fact that scoring was decreasing in the NHL due to a turn toward defensive play. He was the only player to reach that level for all three seasons, and is the only American to ever have three 50-goal seasons.

Following that, he had two 40-goal seasons, the equivalent of 50 or 60 in 1970s, 1980s and early 1990s.

Along the way, he has been the first-team all-star left winger twice, and the second-team left winger three times. He's also twice led the league in plus-minus.

LeClair was a member of one of the better-known lines of our era, the Legion of Doom, along with Lindros and Mikael Renberg. But don't get the idea that LeClair was dragged around on Lindros's coat-tails. Lindros has spent plenty of time on the injury list over the years, giving ample opportunity for LeClair to sink or swim without him.

With critical eyes watching closely, in most instances LeClair actually played better, taking the responsibility upon himself to compensate for the absence of Lindros.

LeClair may not be the best skater, passer, or puck handler in the NHL, but there's one thing he may be the best at: putting the puck in the net.

Claude LEMIEUX

Claude Lemieux may be the most hated player in the NHL. He certainly is in Detroit, after the episode in which Kris Draper was injured on a devastating hit from behind.

There are even websites whose purpose is to spread hatred of Lemieux.

He's a super pest, super pesky, and a super playoff performer. Some people may even call him a super chicken, considering his reluctance to fight on occasion.

Whatever you may hear or think, Claude Lemieux is absolutely fearless. He irritates opponents on purpose to throw them off their game, to make them think about going after him rather than winning.

During the 2000 playoffs, a reporter asked Lemieux about shaking hands after a series—a rather ironic query considering Tie Domi of the Maple Leafs once refused to shake Lemieux's hand. Lemieux gave a fairly lengthy answer, but one thing in his response stuck out: "As mean as everyone has to be to one another to be successful, you must keep that tradition involved in part of the game."

"As mean as everyone has to be to one another to be

successful?" That gives you a little bit of insight into the way Claude Lemieux thinks.

As far as being successful when it counts most, count Lemieux as one of the best in the history of the game. The playoffs are where he shines brightest—and where other players dislike him most.

Before Lemieux ever played a game in the NHL, he had an incredible playoff as a member of Verdun in the Quebec Junior League. In 14 games, he had 23 goals and 17 assists, for 40 points.

The next season, as a rookie in the NHL, he was a late call-up by the Montreal Canadiens, getting into ten regular-season games. In the playoffs, however, Lemieux went nutty again, getting ten goals and six assists, to help Montreal win the 1986 Stanley Cup. Those ten goals were the third-most ever scored by a rookie.

A legend was just getting started.

Lemieux won the Conn Smythe Trophy as the most valuable player in the playoffs in 1995; twice he's led the playoffs in goal scoring; and his 19 game-winning goals are second only to Wayne Gretzky's 24.

And we're not finished yet. Lemieux is one of only four players in NHL history to win a Stanley Cup with three different teams, and only the fifth to do it back to back with two different teams.

During the 1999–2000 season, New Jersey GM Lou

Lamoriello obtained Lemieux back from Colorado, where he had been traded the year after the Devils won the Stanley Cup, in 1995. Lemieux didn't leave on good terms due to a contract dispute, but when it came to winning, it didn't matter to either him or Lamoriello.

During the 2000 playoffs, Lemieux didn't have a stellar year by his standards as far as point production was concerned. He had four goals and six assists in the 23 games New Jersey played, but might have had triple that were it not for a boatload of missed chances and perfect passes that weren't converted. He was only one behind Brett Hull among shot leaders.

If you watch Lemieux closely during the playoffs, you can see just how smart he is on the ice when it counts. He knows when to join the rush, the appropriate time to chase a defenseman and deliver a big-time body check, and when to hang back.

One play in the finals typified his desire to win: After the Dallas Stars turned the puck back up-ice, he back-checked hard, but knowing he couldn't reach the player with the puck, he went right to the net. The player took the shot and just as the goalie made the save, Lemieux reached the net, standing behind Martin Brodeur in case he failed to make the save.

People say all sorts of things about him, but there's one thing nobody would ever dispute: Claude Lemieux is a winner.

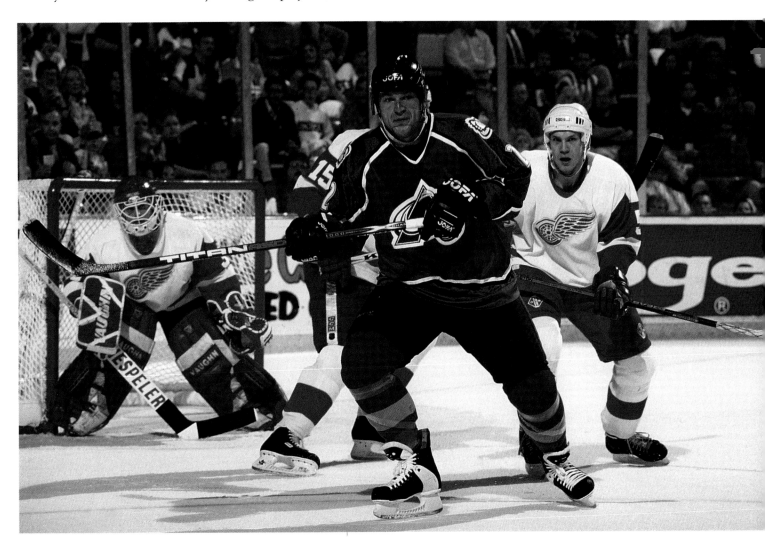

AL MacINNIS

There are several unwritten rules in hockey: You don't pick a fight with Chris Simon, you don't bother with the wraparound on Dominik Hasek, and it used to be that you didn't body check Wayne Gretzky.

Another rule, equally as important, is that you don't get in the way of an Al MacInnis slapshot.

He has shattered glass, broken bones, busted twine, and created trophy-size bruises. Most of all, he has used his killer slapshot to score goals—lots of them.

During an injury-plagued 1999–2000 season, MacInnis became only the fifth defenseman in NHL history to score 300 goals over his career. The others

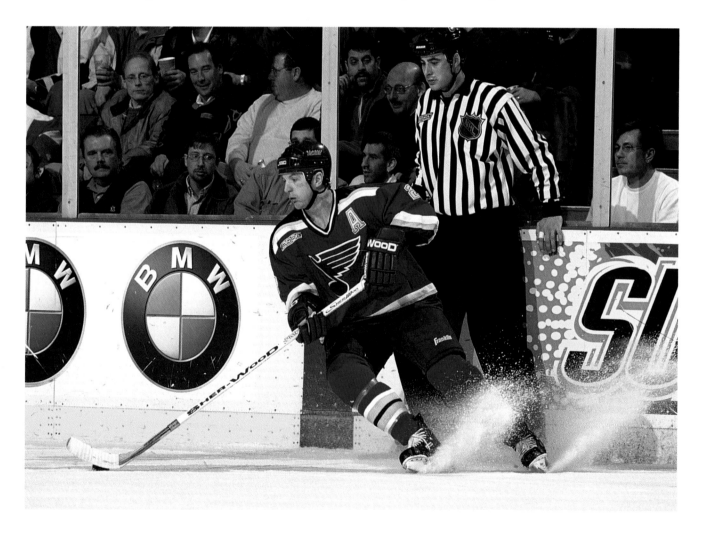

—Paul Coffey, Ray Bourque, Denis Potvin, and Phil Housley—were feared for several reasons, but none of them for the shot that Al MacInnis possesses.

To find a player who could strike as much fear from his shot into opposing players as MacInnis, you'd have to go back to Bobby Hull and the advent of the curved stick.

That shot has made MacInnis one of the best power-play pointmen in NHL history. In fact, if you were picking an all-time best power-play unit, you could do no better than to start with MacInnis on the right point.

Almost half of his goals—145 of 301—have come from that spot. If you've ever seen a power play that MacInnis has been on, it's simple to see the game plan. The other players

have to find a way to get it on his stick. Then they go to the net to try and tip in the puck, or to get a rebound, or to wait perhaps for a fake shot and a pass.

That's why he also has 803 assists during his career, which is something only four other defensemen have accomplished: Paul Coffey, Ray Bourque, Larry Murphy, and Phil Housley. The combined point total of 1,104 also places him fifth all-time among rear guards.

One of the most common questions MacInnis is asked is just exactly how he came to have the most feared shot in hockey. The answer is a little bit of luck and a lot of hard work.

His father was an arena manager, and MacInnis would collect pucks during the winter to shoot in the off season. That's why his shot has always been hard, even as a youngster, but it hasn't always been as accurate as it is now. Earlier in his career, it wasn't just opposing players who were frightened when he wound up from the point, it was his own teammates as well, those daring enough to stand in front of the opposing goaltender. He managed to get it under control over time, without giving up any of the speed.

The Inverness, Nova Scotia, native played 13 years in Calgary before being traded to St. Louis in a deal that saw Phil Housley go the other way. In Calgary, he not only won a Stanley Cup in 1989, but also took the Conn Smythe Trophy as the playoff's most valuable player.

Other career highlights include winning a couple of the hardest shot competions at the all-star game, being named a first-team all-star three times, a second-team all-star three times, scoring 103 points in a season, scoring at least 20 goals seven times, and winning the Norris Trophy as the best defenseman in 1998–99, all the more impressive because he was 35 years old at the time.

MacInnis is actually in better shape now than he was in younger years, a testament to today's better conditioning programs, as well as his own hard work.

The funny thing about MacInnis is that he reacts to every goal he scores as if it's the first of his career. That's because he loves to play hockey. Most of all he loves to let go that shot of his, in all probability the hardest shot in the history of the NHL.

Darren McCARTY

Would the real Darren McCarty please stand up?

One day he's lighting up the scoreboard playing on the top line, the next day he's banging around on the third or fourth line, checking opponents through the boards.

Actually, it's his ability to do both that makes McCarty so valuable. You can stick him on the top-scoring line and know he can help out offensively, dig the puck out of the corner, crash the net, and make more room for the skill players. McCarty, Steve Yzerman, and Brendan Shanahan together form a formidable trio for the Detroit Red Wings whenever they're together.

McCarty is also a player who will stand up for his teammates. Just ask Claude Lemieux, who was on the receiving end of a celebrated revenge pounding after Lemieux hammered McCarty's teammate Kris Draper from behind. That caused McCarty's stock to rise even higher in the eyes of Red Wings fans. There's a computer game with McCarty fighting various opponents, including Lemieux, and you can even buy a Darren McCarty candy bar.

McCarty does spend a lot of time helping others, but it's not limited to the ice. He put together a rock band whose purpose was to raise money for stricken teammate Vladimir Konstantinov and team masseur Sergie Mnatsakanov, who were injured in a post–Stanley Cup limousine accident in 1997. The band was named, appropriately, Grinder.

McCarty also took on another fight, creating the McCarty Cancer Foundation, after learning his father had a multiple myeloma, a form of cancer that attacks bone marrow. Sadly, his father died in 1999, but McCarty continues the battle against the disease.

McCarty is not going to score 50 goals—his career high is 19—but every once in a while he'll show some moves that remind you he was a 55-goal scorer for Belleville in his last season of junior, the 1991–92 season.

McCarty is coming off a rough 1999–2000 season. He held out at the start of the year for a better contract, and then his father passed away. A hernia injury caused him to miss 39 games, which was followed by a leg injury. He only played in 24 games.

McCarty's style tends to lead to injuries, and he's missed more than his share of games because of them. But you could argue that he wouldn't be in the NHL in the first place if it weren't for his style.

McCarty played a big part in the two Detroit Stanley Cup wins, including scoring a spectacular Cup-clinching goal in 1997. He's a character player who's going to come up big at all the right times, and knock his opponents down to size all the time.

And everybody in the league knows that if you mess with one of Darren McCarty's teammates, you're messing with him, too.

Mark MESSIER

The pages in this book are filled with the most fearless players in the game today. What about the most fearless players of all time?

You could go back to the original six, when it was a tougher game, and come up with a bucket full of names. You had to be tough to make it to the NHL in those days or, very simply, you didn't make it to the NHL. Every player had to be a complete player. They had to be able to score, skate, check, hit, be a leader, be prepared to fight, and be intense every single game. It wasn't good enough to be good in just one of those categories.

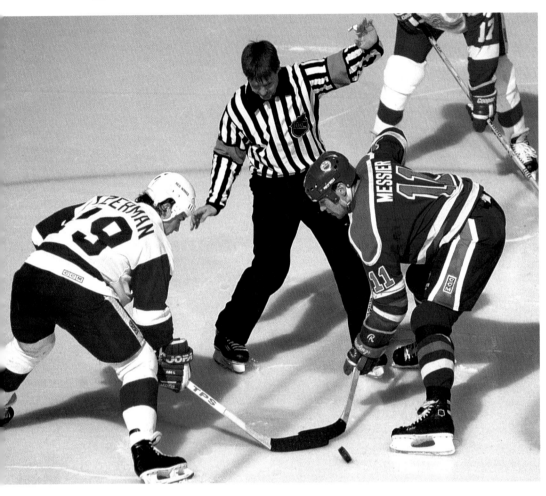

With expansion and the addition of hundreds of players, the NHL entered an age of specialization. Just excelling at any one of those attributes would be enough for a good shot at an NHL career.

One player stands out in the current era as having everything necessary to have been successful in the original-six era, and even manages to go one step further. Mark Messier may not only be the most fearless player of all time, he may also be the most complete player in the history of hockey.

Pretty heady praise, but let's look at the evidence: By watching him for 21 NHL seasons, we know he's one of the best and fastest skaters we've ever seen; we know he can hit and play a tough game; we know he plays both ends of the ice; and we know he's intense every night, because he's been that way every time we've watched him play a game.

We know he's a leader because he's been the captain of every team he's been on: Edmonton, New York Rangers, and Vancouver.

We know he's a winner because he's won six Stanley Cups, including one in Edmonton after Wayne Gretzky was traded to Los Angeles, and another as the leader of the New York Rangers.

Twice, in an era dominated by Gretzky, Messier has won the Hart Trophy as the league's most valuable player. And even while playing with Gretzky, he won the Conn Smythe Trophy as the playoffs' most valuable player.

And we certainly know he can score. Six times he's had over 100 points, and on the all-time list he ranks sixth in goals (627), fourth in assists (1087), and fourth in points (1724).

Finally, we know he can do everything he does in

the regular season during the playoffs. He is second in all-time goals scored (109), second in assists (186), and second in points (295). The leader in each category, not surprisingly, is Wayne Gretzky.

Mark Messier isn't the player he once was, after 21 seasons in the NHL, but that hardly matters. Nobody has ever been the player he once was.

Tyson NASH

One sports journalist's assessment of Tyson Nash wasn't what you would consider complimentary: He said Nash couldn't score, couldn't check, and couldn't fight.

Well, whether that was true or not, there was one thing Nash could definitely do: play on the best team in the league. The St. Louis Blues won the President's Trophy in the 1999–2000 season, and Nash was an integral part of the team, playing 66 games, and earn-ing four goals, 13 assists, and 150 penalty minutes.

Teams need role players to be successful and Nash fits the bill. He's a crasher and banger, one of the more exciting players in the league to watch. His energy might not count in the scoring stats, but it rubs off on his teammates, and that's where it might count in the winning column.

Nash played his junior hockey in Kamloops for the Blazers, a famed Western Canada junior team that produces winners—both teams and players.

He was selected 247th in 1994, in the 10th round by the Vancouver Canucks. When that happens, you think about selling life insurance for a living. Nash spent his days in the Canucks organization in the minors —three years in Syracuse, plus part of another for Raleigh in the East Coast League. When he became a free agent, the Blues signed him and then assigned him to their minor league team in Worcester.

Nash was well on his way to becoming a career minor leaguer, but some players don't give up the dream, no matter what the cost, and Nash is a prime example of that. A year later he was thrilling the fans in St. Louis with his reckless brand of hockey.

Let's make Nash our poster boy for players who came from the depths to somehow make it to the NHL. He isn't going to win any NHL awards, but he fits our mold as a fearless player.

There were some players chosen after Nash in the 1994 draft that have also played in the NHL, most notably Sergei Berezin (256th, Toronto), Richard Zednik (249th, Washington), Tomas Holmstrom (257th, Detroit), Jeremy Stevenson (262nd, Anaheim), Scott Fankhauser (St. Louis, 276th, played with Atlanta), Pavel Torgayev (279th, Calgary), and Kim Johnsson (NYR, 286th). Johnsson was the very last player taken. But many of those players are Europeans, and it's more difficult to determine whether European players can make it in the NHL. Sometimes it's their availability that determines their late pick, while other times it's difficult to assess their

adaptability to a different game and culture. To their credit, they often have good success despite low expectations, although many of those with high expectations fail to deliver on their promise.

But for a North American to make the grade after being chosen as late in the draft as Nash was, it's a little extra special, because they've already been heavily scouted and teams don't figure much on surprises.

So hats off to Tyson Nash and all the other late-rounders who make a go of it.

Owen NOLAN

One of the more memorable images from the 2000 NHL playoffs is that of Owen Nolan standing and screaming down the bench at his San Jose Sharks teammates,

trying to rally the troops who were trying to knock off the number one–seated Western Conference St. Louis Blues.

Mission accomplished. The Sharks, spurred on by their captain and leader, managed to dispense with the President's Cup champs in seven games. Nolan was clearly the star of the series, in more ways than one.

He has a reputation for being a hothead who can fly off the handle at any time. But throughout the series he managed to maintain his discipline, showing his leadership skills. There's a time and a place for retaliation, Nolan said, but this wasn't the time.

Nolan was the first overall selection in the 1990 draft, going to the Quebec Nordiques. He had a terri-

ble rookie season, scoring only three goals. The disappointment was short lived, however. The next year, he scored 42, followed by 36. He missed all but six games the following season with a shoulder injury, but came back with a vengeance in the labor-shortened campaign in 1994–95, scoring 30 goals in 45 games, which projects to over 50 had they played the full 82 games.

The following season, the Nordiques team moved to Colorado and won the Stanley Cup. Nolan's timing was off, however, as he was traded less than a month into the season to San Jose for Sandis Ozolinsh. He finished the year strongly, and put up some good numbers the following season as well.

Then the wheels seemed to come off. Before the 1999–2000 season, Nolan had two years in which he

scored less than 20 goals, 14 in one and 19 the next. Maybe he didn't have top-notch linemates or the right center to get him the puck, but everything seemed to fall into place when the Sharks obtained Vincent Damphousse, and then re-signed him as a free agent.

Damphousse seemed to be the perfect tonic for Nolan, who had a wonderful 1999–2000 season, one of the better comeback seasons in recent memory. He finished second behind Pavel Bure, with 44 goals, was sixth in the league in overall scoring (84 points), was first overall with 18 power-play goals, third with four shorthanded markers, and first in shorthanded points. He also smashed several San Jose scoring records, including most goals in a season and most points.

It's unusual for a player to have his most productive season in his 10th year, but nobody had ever questioned Owen Nolan's skills.

He has a great shot, is an outstanding skater, and is physically intimidating. When you add intensity and responsibility for leadership, Nolan's unstoppable.

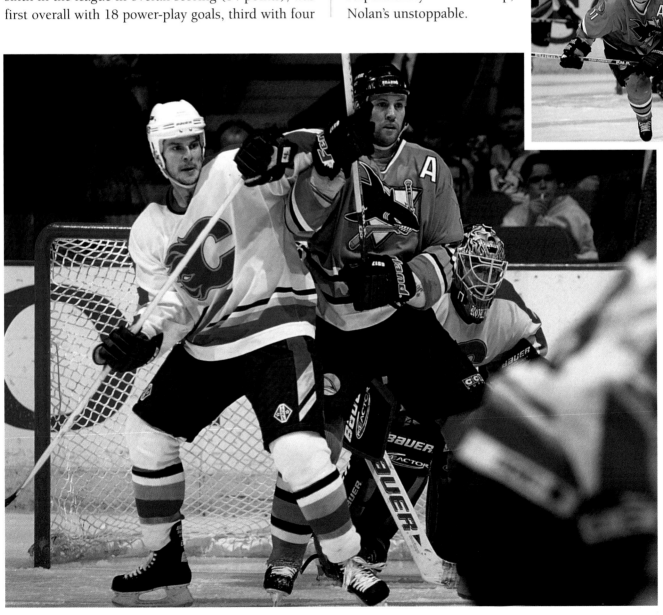

Mike PECA

Off the ice, with his slight physique and glasses, Mike Peca resembles some kind of computer geek, or maybe a mild-mannered newspaper reporter from the Daily Planet.

He must step into a telephone booth to change uniforms, because once he hits the ice, Peca transforms into one of the fiercest competitors in the game. Super Pest, Super Checker, Super Hitter, Super Pain in the Butt—call him anything you like, but make sure you keep your head up.

Peca is considered one of the best hitters in the NHL. Quite a feat for a player shorter than six feet and listed at 180 pounds. Somehow, he knows how to concentrate every ounce of force into his hits, like a boxer who puts all his energy into the end of his fist for a knockout punch.

Because Peca is such a good skater, opponents better look over their shoulders when they go into

the corners, because he can be there in a flash. Otherwise, they'll be lying on the ice wondering if anyone got the license number of the transport truck that hit them. Just a minivan, they might be informed later, but one with good tires.

That skating ability and intensity also contributes to Peca's status as one of the best defensive forwards in hockey. He won the Selke Trophy to prove it, in the 1996–97 season, but he shone brightest in the Sabres' 1999 playoff run, which took them to the Stanley Cup finals.

The Buffalo captain's job was to shadow, check,

pester, or do anything else to neutralize the other team's top scoring threats. First, Peca held Alexei Yashin scoreless, as Buffalo beat Ottawa 4-0. Then he did a number on Jason Allison and the Boston Bruins, especially in Buffalo's rink, where the Sabres had the last change. Mats Sundin and the Toronto Maple Leafs fell next, and then it was on to the finals against Dallas. Mike Modano didn't score a goal for the Stars, and Buffalo fans will tell you that Brett Hull had one less than he was credited with, as Dallas won the Stanley Cup in overtime on a disputed goal in the sixth game.

Mike Peca can also score, which is a bonus for a defensive player—a huge bonus. He's had at least 20 goals in every season that he didn't miss considerable time with injuries, and has a career high of 27 goals and 29 assists, for 56 points, in 1998–99.

Keith PRIMEAU

You might have seen the goal a hundred times if you watch the highlight packages.

You might see it a hundred times more in years to come.

It was well into the fifth overtime, and already the third-longest overtime game in Stanley Cup playoff history. Keith Primeau picked up the puck inside the Pittsburgh zone and snapped it at the net. Penguins goalie Ron Tugnutt probably didn't even see it. Game over, after 92:01 of overtime.

It was a happy moment for the Philadelphia Flyer

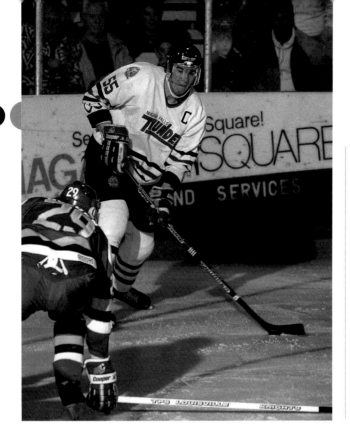

newcomer in a career that has been pocked with controversy and disappointment.

Up to the goal, he was best known for being selected ahead of Jaromir Jagr in the 1990 draft. Never mind that four other players were as well. In Detroit, he was considered a disappointment no matter what he did on the ice. He found it impossible to live up to their expectations.

He was booed in Detroit because he didn't score 50 goals every year. He did score 31 one year and 27 another, but he also scored only nine in 93 games in his first two seasons, and was a colossal disappointment in the playoffs.

He demanded a trade after the 1995–96 season and was booted out of Detroit to Hartford, which

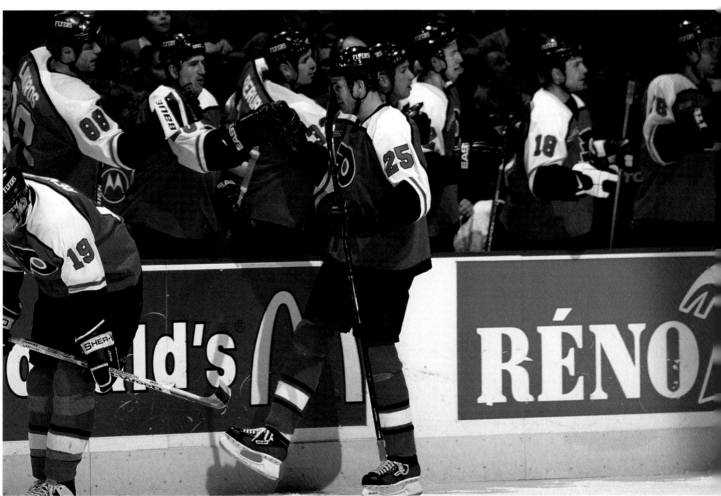

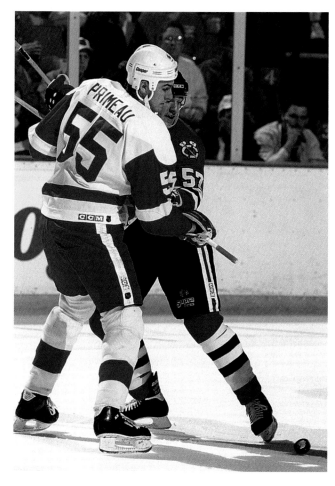

moved to Carolina the following season. He averaged almost 28 goals a season there and was named team captain, but became a holdout to start the 1999–2000 season.

After sitting out most of the year, and not being able to come to a satisfactory contract arrangement with the Hurricanes, he was traded to Philadelphia in a deal that saw Flyer favorite Rod Brind'Amour go the other way.

Primeau was supposed to be the missing ingredient for the Flyers Stanley Cup run, so he was again put into a position where expectations were going to be difficult to meet.

With Eric Lindros out of action because of his concussions, Primeau responded this time. He became a dominant force for the Flyers, centering their top line and helping them reach the conference finals, where they lost to New Jersey in seven games.

Primeau, whose brother Wayne also plays in the NHL, is huge, at 6'5", 220 pounds. When he hits somebody, they remember it—for a long time. He no longer accumulates the penalty minutes he did earlier in his career, partly because his value on the ice is more than it is off, and partly because nobody wants to mess with him.

Primeau's challenge now is to be the dominant player that he was expected to be, and to remain that way.

Chris PRONGER

If you are one of those people who thought Chris Pronger would never amount to much, don't worry about it—you're not alone.

He might have even questioned it himself, playing his early years in Hartford in rather undistinguished fashion. This was the guy one scout had called the best defensive prospect ever? Hmm . . . .

The big 6′6″, 220 pounder from Dryden, Ontario, was selected second overall in the 1993 draft, from the Peterborough Petes, right behind Alexandre Daigle.

Possibly too much was expected of him too soon. It takes a while for young defensemen to mature and learn the game. The Whalers gave up on Pronger after just two seasons, going for the sure thing in a trade with Mike Keenan and the St. Louis Blues. They got Brendan Shanahan, who had a great season in Hartford before demanding a trade the next year.

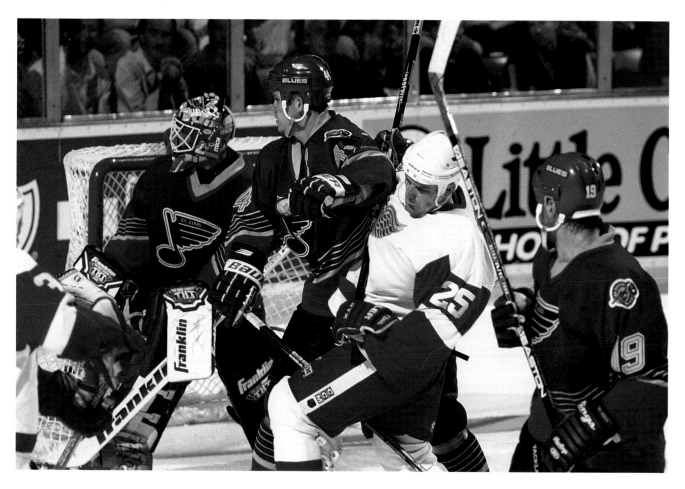

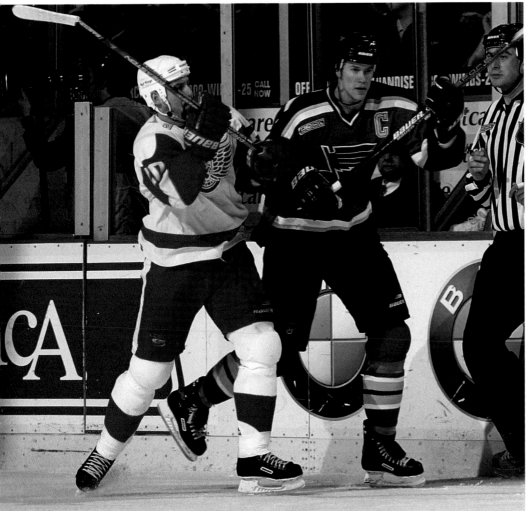

Meanwhile, the St. Louis Blues fans were none too happy about what looked like a one-sided deal slanted heavily towards Hartford. They had lost one of their favorite players for an underachieving youngster who might never be anything more. It was one more step in their quest to run Keenan out of town.

Despite what the fans thought, the trade was probably the best thing that could have happened to Pronger, because in St. Louis he met up with Al MacInnis. MacInnis took on the role of steering Pronger in the right direction when, as Pronger put it himself, "It appeared I was going nowhere."

Those are the words he used at the 2000 NHL awards, where he not only won the Norris Trophy as the best defenseman, but also was named a first-team all-star and won the Hart Trophy as the best player in the league. Pronger was the first defenseman to win the Hart Trophy since Bobby Orr in 1972.

Pronger has become a dominant player on the ice, just like Orr, but in a different way. The St. Louis captain dominates physically, defensively, and offensively at times. He averages over 30 minutes per game. He's on the ice when the team is shorthanded, on the power-play, or facing the other team's top line. He led the NHL in plus-minus in 1999–2000, with a +52.

Pronger is acknowledged as the best defensive defenseman in the game, or perhaps more aptly put, the defenseman with the best defensive skills. That's because he's also one of the best offensively. He had the second-most points in the league by a defensemen (behind Nicklas Lidstrom), with 14-48-62, in 1999–2000.

Typical of Pronger's attitude, he said he would gladly trade the Norris Trophy and Hart Trophy for a Stanley Cup. The Blues were knocked off in the first round by San Jose, after finishing the regular season with the most points by any team.

The Stanley Cup will come to St. Louis, no doubt about it, if Chris Pronger has anything to say about it.

Rob RAY

Rob Ray isn't going to win any scoring titles, isn't going to be on any all-star teams, and doesn't do much on the ice except fight.

Ray did, however, win an NHL Trophy—but more on that in a minute.

A recent poll asked which player was the NHL's best fighter. Nobody came even close to Ray in the results, which is why he is able to remain in the league without having any other notable skills. Any team would like to have Rob Ray in their lineup for his intimidation skills alone, which is why he's spent his entire career in Buffalo.

Ray has spent 2,687 minutes in the sin bin, which

is good for 10th all-time. He has 34 career goals, so he has 79 penalty minutes for each goal scored. Twice he has led the league in penalty minutes: once with 350 minutes in 1990–91, and once with 261 minutes in 1988–89. Twice he's had over 300 minutes in penalties, and six times he's had over 250. In his first year as a pro, with Buffalo's farm team in Rochester, he had 446 minutes.

Ray has been known to lose control and go over the edge. At times, you'd think he had plain lost his mind. He was once quoted as saying he loved to fight Tie Domi of the Maple Leafs, because he loved pounding on his head. Ray's a guy who knows his role, does it well, and doesn't try to be anything different.

During the summer of 2000, the Buffalo Sabres declined to pick up the option year on Ray's contract, making him a free agent, and most likely ending his time with the team. His ice time had diminished,

especially in the playoffs, and Buffalo figured they could get somebody cheaper to fill that role.

At the end of the season, while reflecting on whether Buffalo's decision was the end of the line for him, Ray was quoted as saying, "There's no way you can be bitter about anything that's gone on and be disappointed, because you've lived in a fantasy world for the last 12 years."

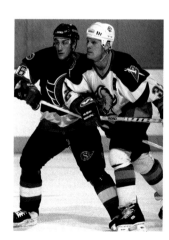

Although there's less call these days for players whose prime skill is fighting, some team is likely to pick Ray up for his character value alone.

So what kind of NHL

trophy would Rob Ray win, anyway? There are no awards for most penalty minutes, or fewest goals, or biggest lunatic. Well, here's a hint: It's exactly the opposite of the noncharitable reputation he's exhibited on the ice. Give up?

It was the King Clancy Memorial Trophy, awarded to "the player who best exemplifies leadership qualities on and off the ice and has made a noteworthy humanitarian contribution to his community."

Maybe because Rob Ray knows the value of a fight, he spends a lot of his free time helping others fight illnesses and disease. He has a summer golf tournament to benefit the March of Dimes. He helps the Make-A-Wish foundation, Children's Hospital, and Roswell Park Cancer Institute. He was the honorary chairperson for Walk America. And he's won awards for his tireless commitment to the community and to others less fortunate than himself.

Robyn REGEHR

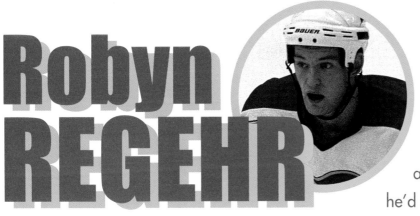

The question wasn't whether or not Robyn Regehr would play hockey again soon, but rather if he'd ever play hockey again.

The highly rated prospect for the Calgary Flames, obtained from Colorado in a major trade involving Theoren Fleury, was driving home from a waterskiing outing north of Saskatoon, Saskatchewan, on the night of July 4, 1999, with his brother and two friends. With no warning, a car swerved into their lane and hit them head on.

Two people were killed in the other car, and all four people in the car Regehr was driving were injured. None, however, as seriously as Regehr.

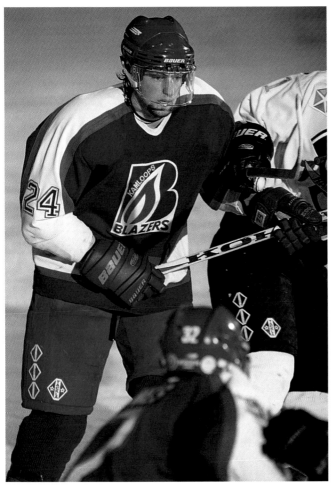

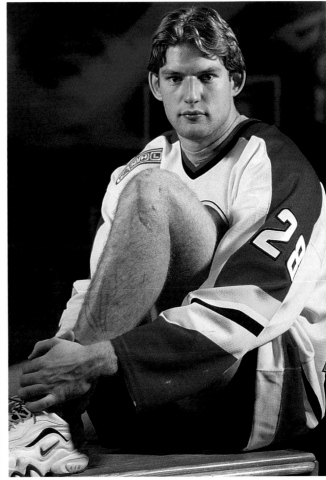

He fractured one leg, and the other was punctured below the knee, cutting off an inch of bone.

It was considered a miracle that Regehr survived the accident at all. After spending nine days in the hospital, six weeks in bed, losing 24 pounds, and having permanent pins placed in his left leg, Regehr began the process of rehabilitation. That was just to walk again, never mind playing hockey.

Fortunately for Regehr, he was in tremendous condition at the time of the accident, and, even more importantly, had a tremendous attitude. There was never any question in his mind that he would be playing hockey again.

Incredibly, just two months and a couple days after the accident, Regehr stepped onto the ice at the Calgary Saddledome at training camp and skated. Even more incredibly, he was sent to the team's minor league affiliate in Saint John for a conditioning stint a few weeks into the season. To cap off the string of amazing events, on October 28, 1999, Regehr suited up for his

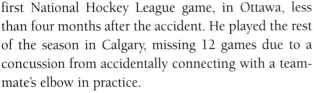

Saskatchewan, and he saw ice for the first time. And then, of course, he almost saw it for the last time at age 19.

Regehr's story has caused considerable attention in the hockey world. He became the first rookie to win the Ralph Scurfield Humanitarian Award, which is awarded to the Flames player who best exemplifies the qualities of perseverance, determination, and leadership on the ice, combined with dedication to community service. Even without his miraculous comeback, the list of charitable events he has been involved in is impressive. "It's important to give back to the community," says Regehr.

That's what a lot of NHL hockey players say, but for Regehr it seems to ring truer, considering his experiences. Those experiences have made him an inspiration to others who have also suffered similar fates.

first National Hockey League game, in Ottawa, less than four months after the accident. He played the rest of the season in Calgary, missing 12 games due to a concussion from accidentally connecting with a teammate's elbow in practice.

Regehr was born in the unlikeliest of places for a hockey player. His parents were both missionaries in Brazil at the time of his birth, and four years later moved to Indonesia for another three years. Regehr was seven when his family returned to Rosthern,

Jeremy ROENICK

Jeremy Roenick is a connoisseur of fine wines. Some people just consider him a fine whiner.

Certainly, Roenick is not afraid to speak his mind. Maybe a little too unafraid on occasion. He's been known to say some outrageous things, such as when he suggested Canadian sportswriters were jealous of him and other American hockey players because they made so much money. If that were the case, they'd be jealous of everyone.

If J.R. never said a word, his play on the ice would do all his talking for him. He's an intense competitor who can deliver a devastating body check as easily as he can score a goal or deliver a perfect pass.

He's one of a rare breed in the NHL who can win games himself, just by his intensity and desire. Consider this statistic from the 1999–2000 season: In

the 36 games the Coyotes won when he was in the lineup, Roenick had 61 points (25-36-61). In their 33 losses he had just 11 points (5-6-11). Incredibly, he was +44 when they won, and −33 when they lost, a swing of 77. The numbers are saying that when the Coyotes won, it was because Roenick scored close to two points a game.

Roenick never played a game in the minors, going right to the Chicago Blackhawks after being selected eighth overall in the 1988 draft, out of Thayer Academy. He played 28 games for Hull in the Quebec Junior League, scoring an amazing 70 points. He even made the second all-star team, despite playing less than one-third of the season.

The Blackhawks called him up part way through the season, and he made his mark right away, scoring 18 points in 20 games. Two years later, he scored 94 points, and then had over 100 points for three consecutive seasons, including two with at least 50 goals and 50 assists.

Roenick is the only American player to have three

100-point seasons, and is one of only four Americans to have two 50-goal seasons. Only Joe Mullen (502) and Pat LaFontaine (468) have more career goals among Americans than Roenick's 374.

Roenick's scoring slowed down after the labor-shortened season of 1994–95, at least by his standards, although scoring had been reduced everywhere. Some said he had lost it, and the Blackhawks traded him to Phoenix for Alexei Zhamnov, Craig Mills, and a first-rounder. As time would tell, the

Coyotes got the better deal.

He's had four productive seasons in Phoenix, including 1999–2000, when his 78 points were good for 11th in scoring. It was also the sixth season in his career that he surpassed 100 penalty minutes.

Jeremy Roenick is approaching 400 goals, 500 assists, and 900 points over his career. If he wants to do a little whining, he's earned it, but it's mostly his opponents doing the whining, because they're the ones who have to play against him.

Patrick ROY

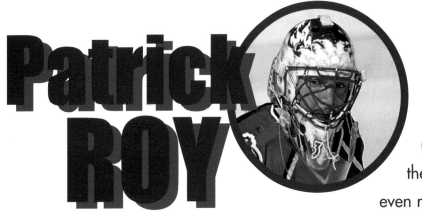

Patrick Roy was having a bad game. That was unusual enough in itself, but the subsequent events were even more shocking.

Roy had allowed nine goals to the Detroit Red Wings in a game at the Montreal Forum, and was finally pulled by the coach, Mario Tremblay. Roy was upset, to put it mildly, that Tremblay had allowed him to remain in the net and continue embarrassing himself. The two stared each other down as he came off the ice, and then Roy went over to team president, Ronald Corey, and told him that he would never play

again for the Montreal Canadiens.

So ended the era of one of the most successful and popular players ever to suit up in Montreal. A strange way to go, considering Roy is one of the best goaltenders in NHL history.

He was traded to Colorado, along with Mike Keane, for Andrei Kovalenko, Martin Rucinsky, and Jocelyn Thibault. Roy didn't waste any time making

an impact, leading the Avalanche to a Stanley Cup that same season.

It was Roy's third Stanley Cup. His first came as a rookie in 1986, and his second in 1993. Both of those seasons, Roy was also rewarded with the Conn Smythe Trophy as the most valuable player in the playoffs.

Roy has been rewarded often, starting in the regular season, where he has won the Vezina Trophy three times, won or shared the Jennings Trophy four times, has been named a first-team all-star on three occasions, and a second-team all-star twice.

Sometime very early in the 2000–2001 season, Roy will become the winningest goalie in NHL history. At the start of the season, he had 444 wins, just three behind Terry Sawchuk.

His regular season accomplishments are one thing, but it's the playoffs where a goalie's worth is truly appreciated. No problem there for Roy, who, along with his three Stanley Cups, has played more games (196) than any goalie in league history, has more wins (121), and is tied with Clint Benedict for the all-time lead in shutouts (15).

Even without the statistics, Roy has left his legacy in more ways than that fateful night at the Montreal Forum. His playing style has spawned a generation of goalies from the province of Quebec, all copying his butterfly style between the pipes.

But more than that, Roy will always be remembered as one of the best goalies under pressure. When it counted most, Roy played his best.

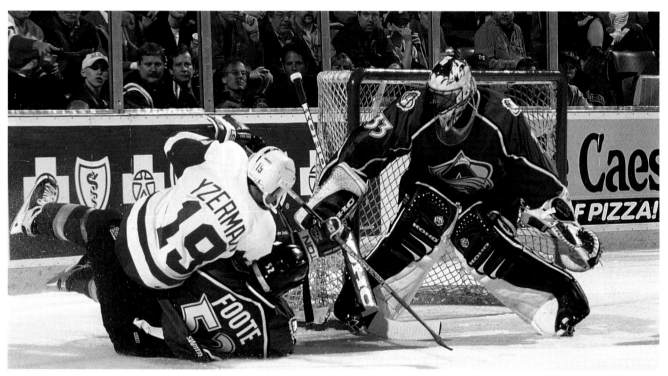

Brendan SHANAHAN

Do you know how rare it is to score 50 goals, 50 assists, and earn 200 penalty minutes in one season?

Rare enough: It's only been done twice in NHL history.

Brendan Shanahan is one of the players to accomplish that incredible mix of scoring prowess and physical intimidation. Kevin Stevens was the other, while playing with Mario Lemieux on the Pittsburgh Penguins.

Shanahan is the most consistently effective power forward in hockey today, maybe even in the past 10

years. Five times he has scored at least 40 goals, and in each of his 13 NHL seasons he's had at least 100 penalty minutes.

The Mimico, Ontario, native played junior hockey for the London Knights, of the Ontario Hockey League, and started his NHL career after being chosen second overall by the New Jersey Devils in 1987, right after Buffalo made Pierre Turgeon the first draft choice.

Shanahan only found the net seven times as an 18-year-old rookie, but even at that age he was already establishing himself as a tough customer. Over the next few years, his stats improved, and so

did his reputation. When he became a free agent, the St. Louis Blues signed him, despite the fact that they had to give up compensation to New Jersey.

St. Louis fans were none too happy about having to give up Scott Stevens as compensation, and let Shanahan know it. He was decent in his first year with the Blues, earning 33 goals and 36 assists, but it wasn't until the next season that he exploded on offense. He had the two most productive offensive seasons of his career in St. Louis, scoring 51-43-94 and 52-50-102, and was named a first-team all-star in 1993–94.

Shanahan eventually became immensely popular in St. Louis, but he clashed with coach and GM Mike Keenan, who joined the team in the labor-shortened 1994–95 season. At the end of that year, Keenan traded Shanahan to Hartford.

Blues fans felt as if they had been robbed.

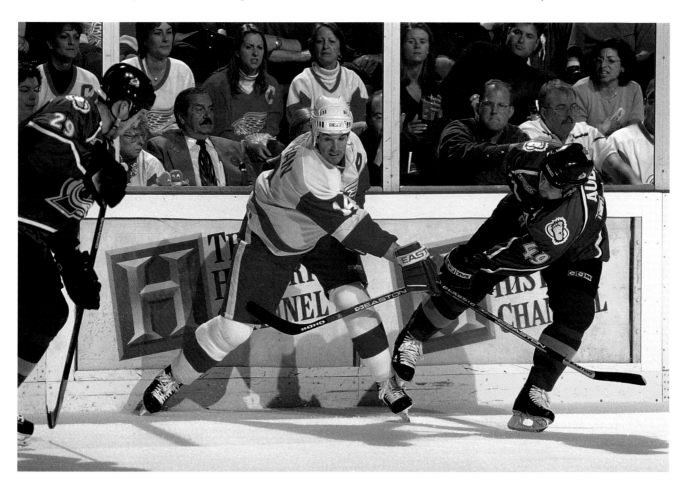

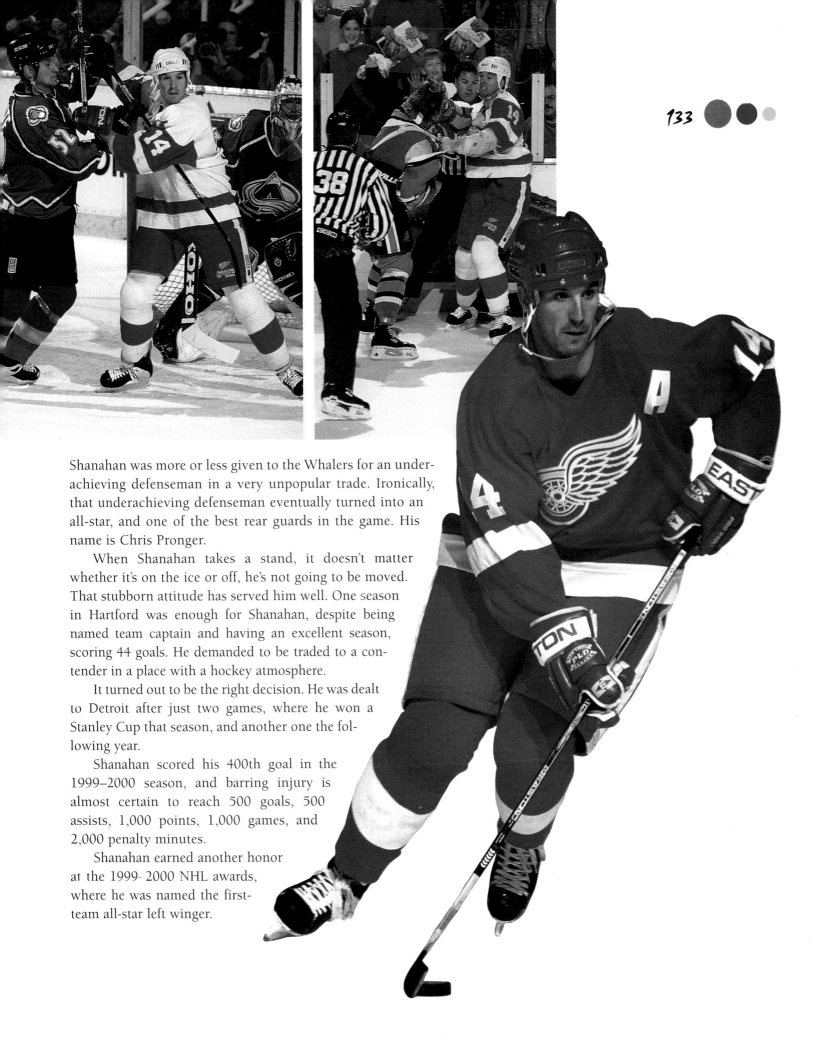

Shanahan was more or less given to the Whalers for an under-achieving defenseman in a very unpopular trade. Ironically, that underachieving defenseman eventually turned into an all-star, and one of the best rear guards in the game. His name is Chris Pronger.

When Shanahan takes a stand, it doesn't matter whether it's on the ice or off, he's not going to be moved. That stubborn attitude has served him well. One season in Hartford was enough for Shanahan, despite being named team captain and having an excellent season, scoring 44 goals. He demanded to be traded to a con-tender in a place with a hockey atmosphere.

It turned out to be the right decision. He was dealt to Detroit after just two games, where he won a Stanley Cup that season, and another one the fol-lowing year.

Shanahan scored his 400th goal in the 1999–2000 season, and barring injury is almost certain to reach 500 goals, 500 assists, 1,000 points, 1,000 games, and 2,000 penalty minutes.

Shanahan earned another honor at the 1999–2000 NHL awards, where he was named the first-team all-star left winger.

Chris SIMON

Chris Simon packs a mean one-two punch. One of those elements actually is his punch. The other is his ability as a scorer.

Simon wasn't supposed to be the leading goal getter for the Washington Capitals in the 1999–2000 season. In fact, he's not supposed to lead any team, at any time. Yet there he was with 29 goals, only 14 short of his entire career total of 43 in seven previous NHL seasons. He's supposed to be the tough guy, the intimidator, the enforcer. The goal scorer? It just didn't fit.

Ironically, one of Simon's sayings used to be, "If you're a crusher and you turn into a rusher, you'll soon be an usher."

So what happened? Mostly, it was a matter of remaining healthy. Simon suited up for 75 games, far and away the most he's played in his eight-year career. Most of his injuries have been back- or shoulder-related, and in the previous three seasons he had played 23, 28, and 42 games. His career high in games, before 1999–2000, was only 65. Simon considers his injuries a product of the way he plays the game. He doesn't hang around the periphery and wait for something to happen; he's in the middle of everything.

Another reason Simon's scoring has risen is that he's already proven his toughness. He was once voted by a major publication as the best fighter in the game. In other words, nobody wants to fight him anymore, unless they

have some kind of death wish. Besides that, he's developed into too valuable a hockey player to be wasting away in the penalty box.

Simon hardly has to fight, anyway, to be intimidating. He's one of the few players who can charge into a corner and get the puck purely on reputation. You could try to get in the 6'4", 230 pounder's way as he takes it to the net, but as many NHL defensemen have learned, it usually doesn't do any good.

Simon, who is from Wawa, Ontario, is half Ojibway Indian, and wears his hair long to honor his heritage. He also spends considerable time helping young native people so they won't make the same mistakes he made while growing up.

He was almost uncontrollable as a teenager, and well on his way to ruin with alcohol and rowdy behavior, when he was traded to Sault Ste. Marie, in the Ontario Hockey League. There he came under the guidance of Ted Nolan, the team coach, and a full-blooded Ojibway himself. Nolan helped Simon turn his life around.

Fast-forward to the 1999–2000 season: Simon didn't have a good start. He had just two goals in the first month of the season, and then just two in the second month. The Capitals were floundering, below .500. Then, when 2000 hit, so did Simon and the Caps. They went 9-1-2 in that month, and Simon scored seven goals. They were both on their way to the top of the standings.

Besides being one of the most fearless players in the game, Simon has also always been one of the most feared. But nowadays he is feared for his hockey prowess as well as his physical intimidation.

Scott STEVENS

Captain Crunch had one of the more memorable playoff performances in recent memory. He delivered some of the most devastating checks I've seen in my lifetime.

Pavel Bure, Eric Lindros, Tie Domi, Tomas Kaberle, Kevyn Adams—all now have personal knowledge of what it feels like to smack full speed into a brick wall; a brick wall by the name of Scott Stevens.

Stevens' hits are the kind that can not only turn a game around, but can turn a whole series around. They can win a Stanley Cup. That was part of the reason Stevens was named the Conn Smythe Trophy

winner when the New Jersey Devils won the 2000 Stanley Cup. In fact, he is the first Conn Smythe winner in history who won as a defenseman without making a substantial offensive contribution.

The New Jersey captain was in his 18th NHL season and his 17th playoffs, a testament to his excellence over a long period of time. Defensively, there may be none better in the game.

Stevens has been a substantial offensive force for much of his career, eight times earning over 50 points. His high was 78 for New Jersey, in 1994–95. In recent years, however, as he's gotten older (he turned 36 just prior to the 2000 playoffs), he has concentrated on play in his own zone.

One incredible stat from Stevens' 18-year career is that he's never once been a minus—not once. In 1993–94, he led the league with a plus 53. His career totals are reaching impressive levels: He's played 1,353 games, good for 20th on the all-time list. He has 2,607 penalty minutes, and 828 points.

In 2000, the New Jersey captain provided a prime example of the kind of leadership that wins Stanley Cups. Ironically, the Devils had been accused in

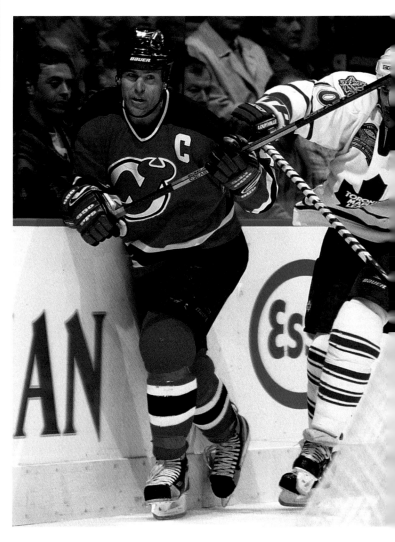

recent years of not having good leadership. But when Larry Robinson took over the coaching duties near the end of the season, he told the team that, in fact, they already had a great leader in Stevens. Robinson drew comparisons with Bob Gainey, who had been a great leader in his years with Montreal, but, like Stevens, wasn't a rah-rah guy who did a lot of screaming and ranting. The Devils took Robinson's words to heart and noted that every time they needed a big play or a big hit or a great defensive play, Stevens was there. Many of the players spoke of Stevens' leadership after the win.

Stevens has probably built up a good enough résumé to be inducted into the Hockey Hall of Fame when he retires. He's played in 10 all-star games, and has been named to the first all-star team twice and the second team twice. One missing piece of the puzzle is the Norris Trophy as best defenseman, which Stevens has yet to win, although he has been runner-up twice. After hoisting the Stanley Cup above his head for the second time, however, Stevens made it quite clear that he'd much rather have that trophy than the Norris.

Besides, without him leading the way, the Devils wouldn't have won in 2000. That's why Scott Stevens was judged not only the best defenseman in the playoffs, but the best player of all.

Joe THORNTON

One minute he had superstar written all over him; the next minute he was super dud.

Now you can just call him Bud, as in budding superstar.

The blond, floppy-locked Joe Thornton more resembled a beach bum than a hockey player, but he carried the future hopes of the Boston Bruins on his shoulders when he was selected first overall in the 1997 draft.

The St. Thomas, Ontario, native went right to the NHL as an 18-year-old and wasn't even close to being the rookie of the year. In fact, it was teammate Sergei

While it appeared that Thornton's rookie season was a disaster, there was still the big picture to consider. The Bruins didn't expect him to win the scoring championship his first season, so they were willing to bring him along slowly. While Samsonov was getting all the raves, Thornton was getting splinters from sitting on the bench, and couldn't help hearing the whispers that it appeared the Bruins had made a big mistake in selecting him first overall.

In his second year, Thornton got off to a slow start, but started coming around in the second half of the season, finishing with totals of 16-25-41. In his third season, he started to show why he was the first selection overall. He led the Bruins in scoring, with 23-37-60, outscoring Samsonov by 15 points. He also led the team in penalty minutes with 87, the only player in the league in the 1999–2000 season to lead a team in scoring and penalty minutes. He was also the second-youngest player (next to Vincent Lecavalier of Tampa Bay) to lead his team in scoring.

Thornton also became only the second player in team history, and the first since the 1924–25 season, to lead the Bruins in goals, assists, points, and penalty minutes.

Thornton is big at 6'4" and 220 pounds, but unlike a lot of scorers of the same size, he plays a tough, physical, intimidating game. He has the complete game, which is why he was selected first overall in 1997.

Joe Thornton may not have got off to the greatest start for his career, but he's making up for it now, and he's just getting started.

Samsonov who won those honors, selected eighth overall in the same draft. Thornton had just three goals and four assists in 55 games. Samsonov had 22 goals and 25 assists.

Keith TKACHUK

The Hockey News has a pet statistic they call the "I.Q." It means "Intimidation Quotient." It multiplies goals scored by three and then adds penalty minutes minus misconducts.

Keith Tkachuk won it three out of four seasons following his rookie year, and might have had the statistic named after him if not for a string of injuries and holdouts.

Big, tough, and mean is one thing, but those qualities combined with outstanding scoring prowess is quite another. That just makes Tkachuk a devastating opponent to defend against.

Twice he has had 50-goal seasons, and twice he has had 40-goal seasons. He is one of only four players in NHL history who have scored 50 goals and had 200 penalty minutes in the same season. Here's a listing of those players:

Year	Player	Team	Goals	PIM
1996–97	Keith Tkachuk	Phoenix	52	228
1993–94	Brendan Shanahan	St. Louis	52	211
1991–92	Gary Roberts	Calgary	53	207
1991–92	Kevin Stevens	Pittsburgh	54	254

The Melrose, Massachusetts, native was drafted out of high school by the Winnipeg Jets 19th in the first round of the 1990 draft. He attended Boston University for a year before joining the United States National team and playing in the Olympics and the World Junior Championships.

Following the Olympics, Tkachuk went straight to the Jets, where it took him just over a year to start making a major impact, both on opponents' bodies and in the scoring stats. In Winnipeg's last year, Tkachuk had 50 goals, then recorded 52 when the team moved to Phoenix, making him an instant hit in the new NHL city.

One thing about Tkachuk is that when he gets hot, nobody can touch him. He goes crazy in the goal-scoring department for weeks on end, like a freight train that can't be stopped. As an example, he once had a five-game goal-scoring streak

in which he strung together fifteen points. Another time, he scored nine goals and 14 points over a six-game period.

Tkachuk is a staunch supporter of the American international hockey efforts, playing for his country several times, including two Olympics. He's also one of the best American goal scorers in NHL history, one of just four to have two 50-goal seasons.

Tkachuk had a rough season in the 1999–2000 campaign, with assorted injuries, and several trade rumors which were mostly the result of his hefty salary. As one of the premier power forwards in the game, he's paid accordingly.

Wherever he ends up, and whatever salary he's paid, one thing you can count on is that Keith Tkachuk will earn every penny of it.

Darcy TUCKER

Darcy Tucker is a mama's boy. At least he was during the 2000 playoffs, when he would visit his family's restaurant in Barrie, Ontario, for a meal before games.

You wouldn't want to call him that to his face, though, because Tucker is one of the toughest players in the NHL, despite the fact he stands just five feet, ten inches tall.

While small in stature, the size of his heart goes way off the scale. Tucker was chosen 151st overall in the 1993 draft, an afterthought by the Montreal Canadiens. He had a prolific junior career, but that didn't impress the pros much, mostly because of his size. Little guys can score in junior, but that doesn't mean they can do it in the pros.

He scored 140 and 137 points in his final two

seasons with Kamloops, and won three Memorial Cups. He was the Memorial Cup MVP in 1995, and led the Western Junior League in playoff scoring for the second straight year.

Tucker went to the Montreal farm team in Fredericton the next year, and proved immediately that size doesn't matter, scoring 93 points to win the rookie-of-the-year award. That earned him a call-up late in the season, and the next year, he was in the NHL to stay. Not that he was impressive at the start, at least in terms of scoring.

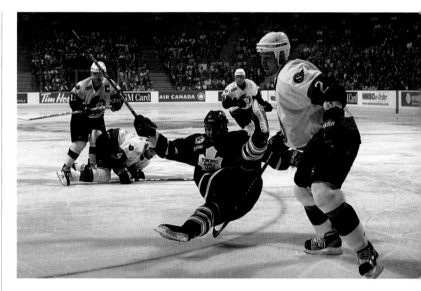

Just as we expected, nodded the naysayers. A tough, feisty little guy, but he's not going to score in the NHL.

Mind you, you're not going to get a lot of scoring opportunities or quality ice-time on the fourth line. In his second full season with Montreal, after just one goal in 39 games, Tucker was dealt to Tampa Bay, where he was so-so the rest of the season.

The next season, on a weak Lightning team, Tucker started to show some thunder. He led the team in scoring and had 173 penalty minutes. Game in, game out, he was the hardest-working player on his team and among the best in the entire league.

Tucker was used to winning, which made it difficult for him in Tampa Bay, although he did everything he could to turn things around. He couldn't do it all on his own, though. When the Toronto Maple Leafs figured they needed more toughness, they made a trade for Tucker during the 1999–2000 season.

Tucker paid immediate dividends, and within a game drew the admiration of the Maple Leaf faithful. He was an instant fan favorite for his tenacity and desire.

During the 2000 playoffs, many of the Leafs struggled, but not Tucker. He was the best player on the ice for Toronto, giving everything he had every time he was on the ice.

That's the type of behavior that makes believers out of nonbelievers. In fact, it's how Darcy Tucker made it to the National Hockey League.

Ron TUGNUTT

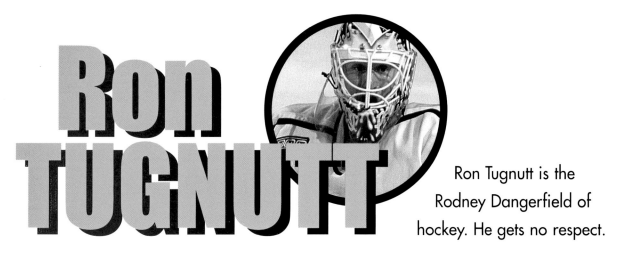

Ron Tugnutt is the Rodney Dangerfield of hockey. He gets no respect.

But Tugnutt doesn't find that the least bit funny. He's had to scrape and claw and fight for everything he's got, and sometimes it still isn't enough for some people.

Tugnutt was drafted from the Peterborough Petes, in the Ontario Hockey League, by the Quebec Nordiques. He was up and down with their farm team for five straight seasons. It was an exceptionally weak team during his time there, and no goalie was going

to be very successful in the win column. In 1990–91, for example, the team had just 16 wins. Tugnutt had 12 of them, despite only playing in 56 games. In one of those games he faced 73 shots, the second-most ever in a regular season game.

The following year, Tugnutt was traded to Edmonton, and then NHL teams played "Who Wants the Goalie" with him for a couple years. He was claimed by Anaheim in the expansion draft, where he performed very well, winning 10 games and losing 15, but he was traded to Montreal the same sea-son. Subsequently, Tugnutt was released and signed by Washington, who kept him in the minors for a full season.

He was signed as a free agent by Ottawa. He played about half the games during his first regular season, and sparkled in the playoffs. Despite the fact that Ottawa lost in seven games to Buffalo, Tugnutt was the story, posting a 1.98 goals against average. He mostly split the goaltending chores with Damien Rhodes in Ottawa, and in 1998–99, Tugnutt posted the best goals against average in the league, at 1.79.

That should have been enough to satisfy the critics, but of course it wasn't. In 1999–2000, Tugnutt was traded to Pittsburgh for Tom Barrasso. The Senators wanted a goalie who would be better in the playoffs.

But Ottawa was knocked out in the first round, while Pittsburgh went to the second round, virtually on Tugnutt's back. He was remarkable, keeping the Penguins in games they had no right to be in. They were outshot almost every game, and worse than that, almost every period. In the first round, they wiped out Washington—the second seed in the Eastern Conference—in five games. Then they gave Philadelphia fits, losing in six games, with two of the losses in overtime. One of those games went to five overtimes.

When all was said and done, Tugnutt was second overall in goals against average, at 1.77, behind only Martin Brodeur, and first in save percentage, at .945.

You think Ron Tugnutt has finally earned some respect? Don't bet on it.

Conclusion

You have to pay the price if you're going to be successful in the NHL. Some players have paid a higher price, and have ended up, well, paying for it.

Look at Eric Lindros. If he's healthy, he's probably the most fearless player in the game. He's suffered six concussions. After five, he made it back to the lineup for Philadelphia in the 2000 playoffs, and promptly received another one from New Jersey defenseman Scott Stevens, who devastated him with a clean check.

Lindros has the potential to be the most dominant player in the game, with his size, toughness, and scoring ability. The problem has always been injuries, all the result of how he plays the game. If and when he comes back, you can expect him to play exactly the same way. He just doesn't know any other way.

It was exactly the same with Wendel Clark, who retired at the end of the 1999–2000 season. His career was plagued with injuries because he didn't know what it meant to play at half speed or not give it his all every time he was out on the ice. Right from the start of his career, critics suggested that there was no way he could maintain that style of play throughout his career. He proved them wrong, and he proved them right.

He played 15 years in the NHL, after being the first overall draft selection in 1985, but only in three of them did he manage to play more than 70 games.

The former Toronto captain endeared himself so much to the Toronto fans that he had three different stints with the team, with short stops along the way in Quebec, the New York Islanders, Tampa Bay, Detroit, and Chicago.

The Toronto fans appreciated the way he played,

and if his body didn't quite match the size of his heart, well, he wasn't going to let that stop him.

Shayne Corson is another player who has paid the price with his body. Eight times during his 14-year NHL career he has played fewer than 65 games. He's battled through every type of injury imaginable, and if that wasn't enough, he also has colitis.

Although he's never been a particularly high scorer—31 goals and 44 assists for 75 points is his career high, for Montreal in 1989–90—he's always been a particularly effective player because of his fire and heart. During the summer of 2000, he signed with the Toronto Maple Leafs.

Gary Roberts also signed with Toronto as a free agent in 2000. He's a similar type of player because he

throws caution to the wind and sacrifices everything he has for the sake of the team. The former 50-goal scorer doesn't put the puck in the net like he used to, but he doesn't ease up either, despite taking a year off for what looked at the time to be a career-ending neck injury.

All of these players have paid a price in excess of the NHL average. That's what makes them so memorable, so adored by fans, and, ultimately, so valuable.